ghosts by daylight

A MODERN-DAY WAR CORRESPONDENT'S
MEMOIR OF LOVE, LOSS, AND REDEMPTION

ghosts by daylight

Janine di Giovanni

ARCADE PUBLISHING • NEW YORK

Copyright © 2011 by Janine di Giovanni

Published by arrangement with Alfred A. Knopf, an imprint of the Knopf Doubleday Publishing Group, a division of Random House, Inc.

All Rights Reserved. No part of this book may be reproduced in any manner without the express written consent of the publisher, except in the case of brief excerpts in critical reviews or articles. All inquiries should be addressed to Arcade Publishing, 307 West 36th Street, 11th Floor, New York, NY 10018.

Originally published in Great Britain by Bloomsbury Publishing PLC, London. A portion of this work originally appeared in *Granta*.

Arcade Publishing books may be purchased in bulk at special discounts for sales promotion, corporate gifts, fund-raising, or educational purposes. Special editions can also be created to specifications. For details, contact the Special Sales Department, Arcade Publishing, 307 West 36th Street, 11th Floor, New York, NY 10018 or arcade@skyhorsepublishing.com.

Arcade Publishing® is a registered trademark of Skyhorse Publishing, Inc.®, a Delaware corporation.

Visit our website at www.arcadepub.com.

10 9 8 7 6 5 4 3 2 1

Library of Congress Cataloging-in-Publication Data is available on file.

ISBN: 978-1-61145-910-4

Printed in the United States of America

For Bruno

(This is my love letter)

CONTENTS

PART ONE

In his sorrow he found one source of relief in war

Tacitus, *Agricola*

CHAPTER I

Beginnings

We arrived in Paris in rainy January, the first week of the new
year, shuffling our feet like little soldiers retreating from battle. The moving boxes and crates had followed us from places
where there really was war—the Ivory Coast, Iraq, Sarajevo
and Afghanistan—and were filled with remnants of the life
that both of us were trying to leave behind.

The boxes were tall and foreboding. Mine were cardboard
from an overpriced shipping agency in London. The movers
came to my Notting Hill flat one afternoon and wrapped my
entire London life in plastic and paper, nearly twenty years
of it sealed away in boxes. They packed everything, even
lipstick-stained cigarettes left behind in ashtrays from a dinner party the night before.

Bruno's crates were more solid. They were wooden and

imposing and came by ship from Abidjan. Together, our combined possessions lined the dining room of our rented apartment on the Right Bank, so there was no room to walk around unless you shimmied between them. Unpacking them seemed a distant chore, impossible, something that would happen far away in the future.

Inside my boxes were pots and pans with burn marks from omelettes that were left unattended for too long; velvet dresses worn once or twice at a forgotten London fancy-dress party; down-filled coats and sleeping bags still lightly coated in dust. There were hiking boots with red mud from Afghanistan; my mother's delicate china tea set; my black-and-white photographs from Africa and the Middle East and the Balkans. There were pieces of a disassembled wooden Shaker-style chair I had bought with a previous boyfriend, ready to be reassembled in Paris, and piles of old, worn linen sheets bought in Ireland and Rome. There were towels and dishes, pie plates with bits of burnt pastry still left on them and hundreds of books.

I had left the flat where I had lived for a dozen years empty except for the bed. That was staying behind; I could not bear to bring it to my new life. I had inherited it from an Irish girl, a banker, who had fled to Dublin with a broken heart, and it seemed time to pass it on again, this time to the blonde German lodger, a solemn psychoanalyst, who was renting my flat.

Also inside the boxes were things that would only make sense to me. Painful stiletto heels which were bought in New York on a whim and worn only once; an ashtray stolen from a hotel in Algeria; some bits of metal shrapnel twisted like an odd sculpture; a packet of love letters—some of them faxes, faded with time—tied with a pale pink ribbon; and two flak jackets with Kevlar inserts to protect the chest and groin and shoulders from bullet wounds.

There were also two helmets with my blood group taped on the front and carefully marked in indelible ink; a nylon bag of medical supplies; packets of the antibiotic Ciprofloxacin; a buddy injection of a liquid opiate that I had stolen from a miserable red-headed American soldier before leaving Kuwait for Basra. There was a satellite telephone and two digital cameras that I had never learned how to use, still in their boxes with the instructions. There was a waxy chemical weapon suit, wrapped in plastic and tied with elastics; an unused gas mask; and maps of Baghdad circled in red at strategic points.

There were eighteen black-covered notebooks scribbled with names like Ali and Bassam and Mona and Ahmed— names of people I had interviewed in what seemed like another lifetime, and my canvas boots, still full of sands from the western desert in Iraq.

Bruno's packing cases were more exotic than mine. His boxes were filled with things Claude Lévi-Strauss might have collected during his long and lonely voyages. There were bits of woven fabric in equatorial colours; long, feathered arrows from Brazil; black-and-white shimaghs from the Middle East; pink-and-white shells from the beaches near Grand-

Bassam, outside of Abidjan; green and red and black beads from Mali; a dried-out starfish that still smelled of the sea; teak tables and mirrors with ivory inlays; brass trunks; a heavy white blanket from Ethiopia; and ancient Buddha heads from Afghanistan and Burma. He had a long cloak from the Tuaregs in the Sahara, and he knew how to wrap it so that he looked, as he put it, like a man from the desert.

There were six brass cups from somewhere in Central Asia. There were lapis lazuli necklaces from Iraq and prayer rugs from Kurdistan. There was a metal box full of photographs which he kept secret. There was his name written in Greek on a gold plate which an old girlfriend, a lawyer, had made for him. And there were rugs from a trip to Afghanistan where we had both met by chance and then dramatically split up, for absolutely the last time, I had thought. We were slowly, and with great tentativeness, lifting our old lives from the boxes and trying to make room for them in this new and frightening life.

Bruno looked the same as he did when I first met him, many years before, in the hotel lobby of the Holiday Inn in Sarajevo. It was in another lifetime, and it was strange, how we met, how two people, two lives collided full force with as much impact as a donkey kick. And because of that chance collision, another life was made, a child was born, and our cycle went on. "Now you both are immortal," someone told him the day our son was born. At the time, still bleary from drugs and pain, and the shock of holding another life in my hands, I did not understand the words. Now I do.

The lobby of the wartime Holiday Inn was an ugly, cavernous space that opened up to the hallways of the eight floors. It was freezing in winter, scorching in summer, and got shelled and shot at on a regular basis. It was positioned in one of the most dangerous front lines of the city, a place we called Sniper's Alley. Journalists, penned up for months and months and growing bored, used to abseil with rope from the top to the bottom of the lobby. There were long periods without water, electricity and heating in the winter, and one season we had to drop red tablets into the water for fear of a cholera epidemic. The food, one of my colleagues once remarked, was worse than his grandfather ate in Auschwitz. We subsidized it with expensive black-market luxuries, or packages of chocolate picked up at the last minute in Zagreb Airport before boarding the United Nations flight that dropped us in Sarajevo for months and months and months.

In the summer of 1993, the second year of the war, Bruno and I arrived from our respective homes in Paris and London to report on the longest-running siege in modern history. He was a cameraman for the main French channel, France 2, and I worked for a major British newspaper. We were young, easily impressed, very green and young enough to have real passion for what we believed in. I believed then, as I sometimes do now, that occasionally what you write or photograph or film can reach someone somewhere, and make some kind of difference. But I did it with more fire in those days.

I had been in Sarajevo since the previous December, but it was Bruno's first time. He saw me, he said, from a mezzanine, which was suspended between the first and second floors. There was a piano on that level, hidden in a corner near the bombed-out side of the building where we were not meant to go because it was particularly visible to the snipers, and sometimes I heard an Italian journalist called Renzo playing ghostly tunes—Schubert, or jazz, which sounded alien, coming, as it seemed, from nowhere.

In those days, we would try to go to the daily press briefing at the UN complex in the old Post Telephone and Telegraph building on Sniper's Alley. If you had an armoured car, the journey was fine and took about seven minutes. If you did not, it was nerve-wracking: stuffed into the back seat of a VW Rabbit with your fellow hacks wearing flak jackets and laden with bags stuffed with computers and cameras, hoping a stray shot would not pierce the metal of the car. In those days, I remembered with frightening clarity the prayers the nuns had taught us when I was small: a slender white book I had forgotten, embossed with gold; prayers about seeking forgiveness before death.

The briefing was at 9 a.m. sharp and I was not a morning person. I usually woke, drank a watery coffee served in a makeshift dining room, grabbed a piece of hard bread and ambushed a television journalist—they always had armoured cars—to beg them into giving me a ride. CNN's truck was always full, and they had the reputation of not helping anyone but their own. The BBC people, however, were more generous, and they usually waved me into the back of their truck. "Get in, hurry up." The back of the car smelled of gasoline from the stores of petrol in tin cans.

The morning I met Bruno was sometime in August. It was hot, but the clouds in Sarajevo lay low and grey, and gave the impression of an autumn rather than a high summer day. After breakfast, I found Jeremy, a fellow journalist, who was kind and funny and who said there was no rush. "Drink your coffee," he said, "then we'll go." We drank the coffee—bitter, black and without sugar—and Jeremy looked at his watch. We grabbed the flak jackets, which accompanied us everywhere. I swung mine over my shoulder, bearing the weight on my right side, and wincing slightly at the pain in my right collarbone, which I had broken twice already. We were headed through the lobby, towards the stairwell that took us to the underground parking lot. Once you got to a car, you strapped in and raced out of the car park as fast as lightning because the entrance lay right in view of the Serbian snipers.

But before we reached the stairwell, someone passed us, clearly in a hurry. I bent to tie my shoelace, then stood up, and saw something out of the corner of my eye. A strange and beautiful man had dropped to his knees in front of me. Both Jeremy and I stopped short. The man held a large camera on his shoulder and was saying something in French—or perhaps in French-accented English—we could not hear because he was whispering. I stared, and Jeremy stared, and the man was also staring, intensely, at me. Eventually, I made out his words: "Don't ever look at me like that!" he said dramatically. He was laughing.

It was a strange moment, one that would ultimately change the entire course of my life. I looked down at this person on his knees. He was slender, almost Asiatic looking, wearing baggy combat trousers and a T-shirt. His boots were highly polished. He had a beautiful, wide smile. He was flirting, and laughing at my reaction. He picked himself up and stood in front of me. He looked directly into my eyes: his were green and unflinching. There was not much for me to do but smile back, weakly, and then turn, embarrassed, and keep walking towards the door.

Jeremy said, "There are cameramen, and there are cameramen. And then there are *French* cameramen." Then Jeremy took my arm rather protectively and we walked to the stairway, leaving the Frenchman—Bruno—still standing there.

I have asked Bruno so many times why he did that, why he fell on his knees, unembarrassed, unencumbered and nimble—and he has always shrugged, or muttered something, never giving me an answer, only sometimes quoting Montaigne about not wanting to know why you loved a certain woman, and if you knew the answer to it, you would love her no more. I asked him for years and years, but I never did find out.

I did not see Bruno again for what seemed like a very long time. I did not see him in the dining room where the reporters gathered to eat humanitarian-aid rice and cheese twice a day, and drink wine from the cave that was left over from the siege. I did not see him during the days as I worked alone with my driver, Dragan, and we moved amongst the buildings where I preferred to do my work in the city—the psychiatric unit of Kosevo Hospital, the morgue where I counted the dead, the presidency building where I went to see the vice president, and the orphanage where I went to hold the babies that nobody wanted.

Every Saturday was my deadline at the Sunday newspaper for which I worked, and I wrote in my dreary orange-tinted room with the plastic-covered windows—the glass was blown out during a mortar attack—and then went downstairs to eat my rice and cheese alone. I worked until 5 p.m., and then went to the Reuters office to file my copy by satellite phone at a cost of $50 a minute, knowing that an editor in London would pare it down and pare it down till nothing was left of it but eight hundred words. At night, I slept on top of my sleeping bag—it was too hot to get inside—and listened to the sound of fighting from the open window. Sometimes, if it was loud enough, it woke me from my dreams.

Once I saw him standing in the mezzanine. He whistled loudly and said something in Spanish. *"Señorita!"*

"I'm not Spanish," I said. I had decided that I would flirt back.

"But your dress is."

In fact, it was a housedress that had been bought in a marketplace in Split, on the Croatian coastline, for $5 during a rare break a few weeks before. It came to my knees and had virtually no sex appeal, but in a place like Sarajevo, it stood out.

"You look like a flamenco dancer," he said, leaning over the balcony. And then: "When can we spend time together?"

"I don't know. I'm leaving for Central Bosnia," I replied.

"We'll see each other," he said. It was more of a statement than a request. Then he was gone.

One Sunday in the middle of August, some weeks after I met him, a time when the rest of the world seemed to be at a beach and no one cared at all about a siege in the middle of the Balkans in a city whose name they could not pronounce, I woke at dawn to a knock on my door.

I wore my cotton nightgown, and I covered myself as I opened the door a crack. It was a Bosnian kid in a soldier's uniform, smoking, with a message from a commander written on a piece of paper. The teenage soldier spoke no English but made a motion for me to follow him. I knew what he was doing. I had been waiting for this message for weeks. I dressed, brushed my teeth with a bottle of mineral water, and ran up a flight of stairs to wake my friend, Ariane.

Ariane was my best friend in Bosnia. Tiny, fluent in three languages, the daughter of a French fighter pilot and a Franco-Argentine mother, she was a champion skier and rock climber. She was curvy, green eyed, and her mouth was generous. She was sexy and smart, and said what she thought, a little too loudly sometimes. She was bossy, and irritated me often. But she was frightened of no man, no woman and no thing. Inside her tiny frame was a very big heart. In time, she became my dearest friend in that city, and much later, as the years went by, we grew older together in Paris. She was the first person to visit me in the hospital when my son was born. Back then, she was in love with a tall French colonel, a UN peacekeeper, and I was having an affair with his friend, a captain from Brittany.

Love in those days was so very easy. It was the last time in my life I would love someone so lightly, without any repercussions, guilt, drama or desperation when the time came to leave. Everything about falling in love during wartime, perhaps because our exterior world was so chaotic, was so effortless. It was almost adolescent in its lack of complication. The four of us—the three French and me—would sit around late at night watching the flares and drinking whisky. The soldiers liked to be away from the confines of the United Nations base whenever they got the chance, and they brought us gifts: ready-to-eat meal packets which included small bottles of red wine. Once a week they would take us to the base to shower. This was the most amazing gift: in a city mostly without water, Ariane and I had clean hair.

Ariane liked to be tanned, and she refused to give up her summer skin just because she was living in a city under siege. Instead, she would sit in a chair close to her open window, naked except for her underwear, wearing suntan oil and sunglasses. She claimed she needed the vitamin D, and she was getting UV rays even if the glass partially blocked them. She did, in the end, get what she would call a siege tan.

"I hate looking like a man," she told me that summer, staring at her jeans and sneakers. We had been going around in flak jackets and helmets, heavy shirts that covered our arms, and trousers. I had not worn a dress in months. So we took a trip to Split, that seaside Dalmatian town that was becoming overrun by United Nations soldiers and humanitarian aid workers and journalists, and stayed for a few days, recuperating. We ate risotto with black squid ink and went to the beach—a real beach—and came back with a handful of cotton dresses we bought in the market, one of which was the so-called flamenco dress. They were knee length and respectable; no cleavage, no legs on show, and we wore them with our dirty sneakers to the daily press briefings. They were just cotton housedresses that Croatian cleaners would have worn, but we felt liberated.

The morning the Bosnian soldier knocked on my door, I could tell that Ariane had spent the night before with her colonel. She looked groggy and sleepy; her eyes rimmed with exhaustion. She always smoked as soon as she woke up and she smelled of cigarettes. On her dresser were a big bottle of perfume by Guerlain, a bottle of suntan lotion and a bottle of whisky.

"What?" she said, a little sharply, hazy from sleep.

"Zuc," I replied, and she was quickly awake.

"Christ," she said. She saw the little soldier gaping at her in her short T-shirt and said, "I'm coming." She knew what this meant. We had been trying to get the Bosnian commander to take us to Zuc for weeks. Zuc was the final line of defence in Sarajevo, where a battle was raging, where young boys were dying and their bodies were rotting in the sun.

Ariane picked up a pair of shorts from the floor, grabbed her flak jacket—she refused to wear a helmet—and said she needed coffee and another cigarette. Next we woke a photographer who lived next door, an Italian named Enrico who looked like a young Robert Mitchum and who wore an MTV sticker on his helmet as a way of bringing some humour into the blackness of this place, and then picked up another friend, Chris from Reuters, before heading out the door in a pack. Everyone was smoking, carrying our flak jackets, not sure what we were going to see, what we would feel, in less than an hour on the front line.

And this was the day, a bright, shining August morning in the Balkans, that I was to meet Bruno again.

CHAPTER 2

Bruno

There were green and yellow butterflies on Golo Brdo, a place northwest of Sarajevo whose name meant Naked Hill in the Bosnian language. And they were big butterflies, floating high in the stagnant air. When I was a small girl, my grandmother had told me that butterflies were the spirits of the dead, of people we loved, who had come back to give us a message, something secret and special that the living were unable to tell us.

And during those long, hot August days, there were dead men on Naked Hill. Most of them were very young. They were soldiers, they had been killed and it was too dangerous to remove their bodies. And so they lay where they fell, in the shimmering heat.

The men who came down from the trenches for resupply

every few days said the smell of the dead wafted down into the trenches where the living cowered, waiting for the next round of gunfire. I did not know what the dead smelled like when they rotted in the sun, but a year later, in Rwanda, I would understand it: I would see rows and rows and rows of bodies, the dead, mothers holding their children, stiffened by rigor mortis, fathers with their eyes melting from the heat, and I would remember again Naked Hill.

That summer day in Sarajevo I did not know what we would see when we finally reached the top of that hill. And so I was afraid. Fear, I decided as I climbed behind the sturdy little body of Ariane, my sneakers sliding on the rock, is always in your stomach. It's a little bit like love: it freezes the guts, despite the heat.

The dead on the hill were Bosnian government soldiers, defenders of the city, mown down by howitzers, tank fire, shredded by mortars, run down by rifle fire. Those soldiers had been boys not much younger than me, singing U2 and Red Hot Chili Peppers songs. Like me, they wore sneakers and blue jeans. They did not have uniforms because before the war there had been no army. They had begun to fight to defend their streets, their neighbourhoods and their families.

It was high summer, and the orchard groves outside Sarajevo were lush with fruit trees: plums, apples and pears. In another time, the local women would be picking them, boiling them, preparing them for jams or *šljìvovica,* the heavy brandy that Bosnians love to drink. Maybe now it was what the soldiers were eating. Plums, apples, pears, fallen from the trees, eaten before they died.

It was a desperate front line, this place known as Zuc, and a place where the men who went knew they would probably die. Sarajevo was already blockaded on the southern and western side. Zuc was the last stronghold keeping the Serbs from tearing through and marching straight down to the city centre; if in fact what they wanted was to take the city—most of us were not even sure that was what they really wanted. The war seemed to be much more about terrorizing civilians.

It had been ferocious for weeks, and we had sat in the city waiting for news. Every day Ariane and I walked to the army command and sat with a lawyer turned commander, and petted his dog as he woefully told us how they were losing the war, and the most devastated front line was Zuc.

"We'll go with you," we said. "Take us with you."

He shook his head. "It's so dangerous. And you're *girls*."

"We're reporters."

"It's dangerous for everyone. Why do you want to take such a risk?"

Eventually, though, we wore him down. Ariane and I, combined, had that effect.

The Bosnian troops had the height, but no weapons. The Serbs had everything: machine guns, pistols, anti-tank grenades. They had uniforms and food. They had numbers and strength. And since no one in the West was doing anything to help the weaker party, and the Bosnians were crippled by an arms embargo, it was David against Goliath.

I remember my friend P., a fighter, telling me how their military operations meant taking guns off dead soldiers. What does fighting mean? What does it mean when you go into battle? Does it mean aiming your gun at another soldier in a trench, or does it just mean staying alive long enough to steal someone else's gun? P. told me about the dead he found facedown in a small, muddy river, and how sick he felt, how guilty and sickened he felt, turning them over and taking their guns. "Maybe I would know them," he told me years later, his hand over his face. Shaking. The memory of war, the worst of it anyway, never goes away.

Now, they had to win Zuc. If they lost it, it was the end of their city.

It was already hot when we left Ariane's armoured car at the last Sarajevo position and began to climb, up through the orchards, up through the butterflies. I heard bees and the buzzing of flies. I thought of my violet-eyed Italian grandmother, dead many years, and how she liked to sit in a chair in my parents' garden watching the birds, and how she would never let me swat flies or kill spiders. "You might come back as them someday," she would say.

We sweated as we climbed. Ants circled my ankles. The dirt was red, like Africa. Far, far away, in Geneva—not really so far, only two hours by plane, but it seemed to be another life, another dimension—diplomatic talks were taking place between political and military leaders. Two days before, on a Friday night, General Ratko Mladic, the Bosnian Serb military chief, had declared a ceasefire.

But Geneva meant nothing to us. And ceasefires were a joke, a chance to kill more. We didn't believe in talks any more. The war was more than a year old, and by the time we climbed that hill that morning, half a million people had been cleared away from their homes. American F-16s screeched over the skies of Sarajevo from time to time, and we would run to the windows to look, hoping for something. But they did nothing: they were there to patrol Bosnian air space for Serb military flights. They were not there to bomb, to save the Bosnian people. That would not happen for two more years, when many, many people were dead.

So I climbed, in the heat, my jeans already sticking to my legs, my white sneakers—Keds, the same ones I had worn as a child—getting cloudy with dust, my flak jacket clinging to me. There was a lump of bitterness in my chest that would not go away and, though I didn't know it yet, would be with me for a long, long time. I had been brought up to believe that good prevails over evil, that the good men wipe out the bad men, that the strong should protect the weak. The war in Bosnia showed me, very quickly, how wrong I was.

In the trench were the youngest soldiers. We gave them cigarettes and chocolate. Their eyes were blank, glazed, frightened. I did not ask them how old they were, because once I had done that, late at night, in a trench with a soldier in Central Bosnia. He was on guard duty, and he was frightened.

"How old are you?" I said.

He turned to me quickly, defensively, face dark and closed. He laid down his gun. "I'm nineteen."

Then he turned back to watching the darkness, the hills

around us. After a while he said in the softest voice: "I know what you were thinking."

"What was I thinking?"

He paused. "That I won't live another year. Is that what you meant?"

I was glad for the dark, glad that there were no stars in the sky, glad, for once, that there was no electricity. I was embarrassed that my face felt warm, that he had caught me in the truth. It was exactly what I had meant.

He was a soldier on the first front line. There were hardly any soldiers in his unit. That morning, around dawn, I had seen the dead body of a man wearing pink socks and no shoes in the back of a pickup truck. The day before I had noticed an old school bus packed with the youngest soldiers I had ever seen, their faces pressed against the windows, leaving puffs of breath on the glass, with a sign in the window: DEFENDERS FOR JAJCE. Jajce was another brutal battle, and another city, once the home of Croatian kings, that the Bosnians were losing. I wondered, when I saw them, their white, tightened faces, how many of them would die there.

I had never thought so strongly of death before Bosnia. But then I saw how life leaves the body so quickly, the breath removed, the corpse left still, empty.

"I wasn't thinking that," I told that young boy quietly. He did not answer. He knew it was a lie.

Now I never asked their ages. I asked them what they did. They were all students. They all had messages for me to take to their mothers, their girlfriends; they wanted to know what was happening in Geneva, in New York, with the United

Nations, with the world. They wanted cigarettes, always cigarettes: something to put in their hands instead of guns.

On the hill above me, Ariane was moving towards the trench. In the distance was a Serbian flag. That's how close we were.

"I played football with one of those guys in that trench," one told me. Another said his sister's boyfriend was fighting on the other side.

We smoked. The sun rose hotter. By 10 a.m. we were getting shot at. The pop of gunfire always sounds at first like a toy. Then it gets more dismal. Then you get more frightened. Then you lie down and cover your head, like a child going to sleep.

"Some ceasefire," said the commander, Kristanovic. He was a friend, someone I met occasionally in some black-market bar and drank whisky with. He was blond and had lived in Germany for some time. When the shelling started, we sat tense for a while, then he grabbed the soft flesh of my arm, above the elbow, hard. They always did this, commanders. They did not mean to hurt you, but sometimes they left bruises in their effort to get you out of the way. He turned me towards him: "We go now, or you stay here for three days. No moving after that."

A mortar fell.

Ariane looked up. "Your call."

Three days in a trench, without communications. I had to call my office on Tuesday. If I didn't, I would lose the slot for my Sunday paper, and what was the point of risking our lives for no story?

"Back, I guess . . . ," I said, but I was unsure. The feeling in my stomach said that we should not stay. There was nothing more to be gained for us. But the other feeling, the one coursing through me, was to stay with the soldiers until the end.

Another mortar fell, a dull thud. We turned and ran, Kristanovic holding my hand and pulling me after him, jumping over rocks. I turned behind me to look at the soldiers, already in position, trying to memorize their faces.

"Now!" Kristanovic said, yanking me, grabbing my shoulder. Another mortar fell, this one closer, and he pushed me onto the ground and we all lay flat in the dust and the grass. Then we were running again, and then Chris, the Reuters photographer, said, "Shit!" as he dropped his camera.

"Leave the camera," the commander said. But Chris ran back.

I still have those pictures. Many years later I would look at them and see Ariane in her shorts running down the hill and me behind her in a helmet. Both of us look very young. I would also see something that I did not perhaps see that day: we do not look sufficiently frightened, even though most of our footsteps were being followed with shots. We look like we were coming home from a picnic in the mountains, two young girls, a bit dirty, but behaving normally, aside from the flak jackets and helmets. What was wrong with us that we felt nothing that day, other than sorrow for those boys? Why did we not think that one of those hot mortar slices could dig into our arteries, or slice off a leg, or that we could have stepped on a mine or got shot in the back by a sniper? What part of our brain had ceased to think of these things?

And that perhaps was the most frightening thing of all.

The ability to feel nothing, to be so far away, so removed, from the most profound fear.

I came back from Zuc that day slightly stunned, and dirty and thirsty and longing for tea and a bath. Neither was available. There was a scratch down my cheek and my knees were bruised from crouching. Instead of the bath, I was going to go to my room to think, to write, to lie on the bed and stare at the ceiling. I was thinking about the soldiers I saw in the trenches at Zuc; about the way the light fell between the leaves of the trees as we ran down the hill; about how the commander had taken my hand and said, "Either you leave now or you stay in the trench till the fighting stops."

We were all coming down, weaned off the adrenalin, the strained moments of the first mortar falling. I will always remember the way a mortar sounds like a whistle. And I will never be able to watch fireworks again. Once, many years later, I was on a boat parked in a harbour in Italy on Ferrogosto, the high summer holiday celebrated by the Italians. The fireworks went off at midnight, after the lavish dinner, and everyone else cheered and climbed the mast and jumped up and down on board. But I was huddled as far away from everyone as I could, unable to bear the noise breaking in the sky. It reminded me too much, too painfully, of Sarajevo.

That afternoon, I pulled off my flak jacket and headed towards the stairway but someone was calling me. The man who had fallen on his knees in front of Jeremy and me was sitting at a plastic table in the lobby with the same kind of ease as if he were in a bar in Paris. It was Bruno. He was with a Bosnian girl, an interpreter, with long hair and glasses. There were a bottle of rosé and two glasses in front of him. He was entertaining the girl. She was laughing. Then he was in front of me. "Have some wine!" he said. He stood so close I saw that his eyes were truly green, slanted, with flecks of gold. He was smiling and relaxed. He had the wonderfully confident air of someone in Provence on a summer's day.

I touched the scratch on my cheek. I did not want wine, or jokes, or someone smiling at me. But the man, who looked so small, lifted me into his arms and carried me over to the plastic chairs. The pretty Bosnian girl was laughing.

"You need a glass of wine," he said, and brushed the dried mud off my flak jacket.

And, like that, we fell in love. One grey and hot afternoon a few days later, I crossed the river to interview refugees in the Egyptian battalion side of Sarajevo and he was there, asleep on a wall, his camera next to him. I drew close and saw how delicate the bones of his face were, how beautiful. I thought I had never seen anyone as arresting. As I hovered overhead, leaving a dark shadow over his sleeping form, he opened his eyes. Smiled. "I thought you were an angel," he said.

That love story lasted a week. Then Bruno left for Paris.

He had a girlfriend there, a beautiful and elegant blonde woman who worked in advertising and had no idea of my existence.

I had a boyfriend, whom I loved, that apartment we

shared—decorated with Moroccan rugs and lamps we had bought together in Marrakesh—and an entire circle of mutual friends. But if I loved him so much, why was I always running away to Bosnia? And why, when he flew to Zagreb one wintry day and asked me why we could not get married and have children, did something inside of me recoil? Not at him, because I loved him. But the notion, the expression of confinement, meant death to me, the end of freedom.

Did Bruno and I see this in each other, this resistance to conventionality? One morning, very early, he went back to Paris, leaving me asleep in my room in Sarajevo with a note that said, "I won't lose you," some tins of food he no longer needed, and some Power Bars. I knew where he was going— to the south-west of France on holiday with his girlfriend— and I felt no jealousy. This was his life. And I had mine.

As he crept out in the near dark—someone had knocked on the door and he called out: *"J'arrive!"* and jumped out of bed—he kissed me lightly on the forehead and said, "Take care of yourself. No risks." Years later, he would add something to those lines: "The best journalist is the one who stays alive to bring back the story."

Then he was gone.

Weeks passed in Sarajevo, and rumours that the city was on the verge of falling to Serbian forces were rife. We did our work skittishly, listening to the short-wave radio, desperate for information. And we tried to live. Ariane grew browner from her window and I grew bored of the stalemate of the war. One day, a message came from a French reporter called Aubry, a wry woman with short dark hair and freckles who worked at France Television with Bruno.

"Hey you," she called down to me from the mezzanine of the Holiday Inn. "I've been looking for you for days. Bruno is going crazy trying to reach you."

She ran down the stairs to give me a number to call, and I went to the television centre at the end of Sniper's Alley, where all the TV journalists worked, to borrow a satellite phone from the European Broadcast Union, who always took pity on those of us without phones. I got through to Bruno's office in Paris, and someone passed him the phone. I could hear him breathing over the crackle of the satellite connection.

"This is not fair," he said at first. "Where were you?"

He said he had come back from the south-west of France, where he had surfed. He had tried to find my newspaper to read my stories, but it was sold out. He went to three newsagents before giving up. And his girlfriend wanted to know why he was so frantic to buy a newspaper in English.

His intensity surprised me. "But I thought we would never see each other again," I said. "I thought you left, and that was the end . . ."

"Listen: I want you to come to Germany next weekend. I'm filming in Stuttgart. Can you make it?"

I held the receiver between my hands, trying to hear him amid the noise of the television centre. Someone sat at a desk in front of me listening to his walkman. Another reporter was waiting impatiently to use the phone. A producer from

ABC was motioning me to move out of the way. I tried hard to concentrate.

"But if I leave and Sarajevo falls when I'm gone . . . I won't be able to get back."

"It won't fall," Bruno said persuasively. "Come to Stuttgart."

"I'll try."

"No, don't try," he said "just do it." The finality of his tone was comforting—he believed this was the right thing to do.

I decided then that I would go.

"It's your choice," Ariane said later with a slight disapproving air. "But if I were you, I wouldn't do it. It's too much of a risk."

"But I have to," I told her. "I don't know why, but I do."

She shrugged again, and turned back to her book and her cigarette.

I disappeared a few days later, and told no one but Ariane, who along with Didier, another French reporter who shared our "office," was in crisis mode—storing water, petrol and fuel for the generator in case the city fell. She drove me to the airport in her armoured car. I took a UN flight to Ancona, Italy, a train journey to Rome, a flight to Munich, a connection to Stuttgart. It took eighteen hours and cost around a thousand dollars. But I did not care about the expense. I was earning money and putting it in a bank account in London. I had nowhere to spend it. I did not have a normal life or normal bills to pay. There were no restaurants to go to or clothes to buy in Sarajevo.

I got off the plane in Stuttgart, carrying my flak jacket, my polka-dotted Croatian housedress and my dirty Keds sneakers. Bruno was waiting nervously at the gate. When he saw me, his eyes looked wet. He picked me up and spun me around.

We stayed in a small wooden hotel and slept squished together in a twin bed. I took a shower that lasted an hour. We went to an outdoor swimming pool and I dived off the highest board. He hid in the crowd and watched me. After, we walked in the forest and lay down on the dirt in between the ferns.

I went back to Sarajevo and he went to Kurdistan to live with the Pershmerga, but he hiked for days to deliver a love letter by fax to me. There was a drawing of a mosque on it— he wanted to meet in Istanbul. I put the fax in a box. The affair seemed impossibly doomed, but I had fallen in love with this strange, spontaneous man.

Then, purely by chance, his girlfriend found out. She went—quite understandably—nuclear. Bruno and I met in Paris one weekend and tearfully ended it with cups of hot chocolate on the Boulevard Montparnasse. It was autumn, and I wore a grey jacket and a long scarf. He picked at the fringe at the end of it and explained it was for the best. Then he took off on his motorcycle, to see his brother in Brittany. "I'm sad," he said.

"I'm sad too," I answered.

When I told Ariane, she snorted. "Coward. He could have left her for you, but French men never do." As for the hot chocolate, she added in an annoyed tone, I might as well have rubbed it on my thighs. "That's where it's going to go anyway." She took me to a party that night in the countryside outside Paris and told me to forget him.

I thought about him for a very long time, and then I forgot him. Once, a few years later, I found his number and I rang him but he said, "I can't talk to you. Not now, not ever. I don't want to remember." And I thought, as the Arabs say, *makhtoub,* it is written.

So we said goodbye.

After that, both of us continued to roam, lost in the world.

For many years, we did not talk, did not speak, did not email or text—it was long before those days of easy, constant communication, even before the days of cell phones—and did not write letters. Bruno was an honourable man and he had promised his girlfriend he would never contact me again. I have a vague memory that at one point I rang him again, years after the hot chocolate, and he answered the phone, heard my voice, and put it down. But that also might have been a dream.

The fax that he sent me from Kurdistan had the words "But one thing is certain—they will meet again!" and a drawing of a mosque with a minaret tower. It was now faded, and went into the bottom of an old shoebox. Other people came and went, and then it was five years after we had fallen in love in Sarajevo. The war was over, reconstruction had begun, corrupt politicians had taken over the government and vast amounts of Western money poured into Bosnia. Other wars had exploded elsewhere in the world. I went to Africa, to Asia, to the Middle East, and back again and again to the Balkans.

I put my Sarajevo war notebooks on a shelf in my cupboard, and I saw them every morning when I dressed. I wanted to forget about Bosnia, to say goodbye to that story, that section of my life, but it was always there, a wound that would not heal, no matter how hard I tried to repair it. And one day, when I was preparing to go on an assignment in Algeria at a particularly dangerous time, I found a name in one of my notebooks: BRUNO.

Bruno loved Algeria. He had done his best work there, he told me. And so I rang him, and a secretary answered the phone and gave me a cell number. It was the first time I had rung a cell phone. He answered, and I could hear wind behind him. He was on a ski slope, in the Alps.

"Ah," he said, and his voice sounded infinitely sad. "It's you. I would recognize that voice anywhere." He was filming while skiing backwards and had a twenty-eight-pound camera on his shoulder. And yes, he had contacts in Algeria. He had a friend who would "guard you with his life." He suggested I come to Paris as a layover, and we could have dinner and talk about working in Algiers.

"Did you marry? Do you have children?"

No, he said, he had never married. A few weeks before, he had left his girlfriend, the same one, after nine years. He was broken-hearted, but he felt he had made the right decision. He wanted to know if this was why I had called him.

I did not know about his girlfriend, I told him. I assumed

he was married with five children. I said I was sorry. He said he would meet me at the airport in a few weeks' time.

It was June, and I saw him as soon as I came out of the gate into the arrivals hall of Roissy Airport. He looked older, and smaller. Thinner. Deep lines creased his forehead. He took my backpack and told me I looked beautiful. I had cut my hair short, like a boy, and dyed it black. The back of my neck was exposed, and I remember that he touched it when he kissed me.

"Do you mind a moto?" he asked. I thought he meant a scooter; instead it was an enormous BMW motorcycle. I had never been on one before, and he told me to go to the bathroom and change out of my dress. On the motorbike, he reached behind, leaving one hand on the handlebars and put the other leather-gloved hand on my thigh as he drove. He wove in and out of traffic, in and out of lines of cars stalled for miles.

He took me to La Coupole, the enormous 1920s art deco brasserie on Boulevard Montparnasse, with tables pushed close together and waiters who make a show of bringing your champagne, and he asked for a booth and ordered for us both. Downstairs in the bathroom, I changed back into my black-and-white polka-dot sundress, and tried to wash my face. When I came back, he was smoking and he told me again I was beautiful. "Like a Madonna."

I sat close to him, and we ate steak tartare and frites. He ordered Sancerre. I can't remember what we talked about but it must have been about the years that passed between us.

I had a small bag with me and I remembered when I was packing in London, wondering where I was going to stay. I had not booked a hotel, but I had not assumed I would stay with him. I said, "Can I stay on your couch?" and he laughed.

He handed me a helmet and in the pale heat of a summer night, he drove to the Pont des Arts and led me by the hand to the edge and kissed me. He said, "It seems we have not lost our desire for each other." We drove to his small apartment on the Boulevard Beaumarchais and I climbed seven flights up the stairs after him, he with my bag and his helmet. I did not sleep on the sofa.

We had breakfast in the Café Bastille. I was anxious about my trip, anxious about the danger that lay ahead, the fact that I knew no one at all in the country, and that a reporter in Algeria had been killed the week before. He said, "What are we going to do about our relationship?" and, distracted, I replied: "What relationship?"

He laughed. It became a joke between us for many years. The detachment. The inability to commit. The damage. *What relationship?*

He drove me to the airport and bought me a glass of champagne in the lounge. "To work," he said and clinked my glass. "And to us."

On the way to Algiers there was a storm. The plane shook and wove like a toy and I was frightened. At the gate, there were half a dozen government bodyguards waiting for me, sent by the Ministry of Information allegedly for my protection, but they were really there to spy on me. They made me feel agitated and claustrophobic. But my room in the old Hotel St. George was faded and lovely, and I imagined the days when General Eisenhower used the hotel as his headquarters during the desert campaign of the Second World War. My room was on the ground floor and opened onto a scented rose garden, and I ate my dinner in an enormous dining room, alone, huddled over my notebooks.

I had come to Algeria to report on the dirty war, the killing between Islamists and the government, but it was a different conflict from Sarajevo, or the other places in Africa where I had been working for the past four years. There were no other reporters or aid workers, no camaraderie, no one with whom I could share ideas or secrets or glasses of whisky late at night. There were no front lines, just the shadowy intuition of constant danger. I stood with the doors open looking out to the garden and felt very alone. I was not sure how to write, or what to write. I had Frantz Fanon's *The Wretched of the Earth* with me, but when I tried to read at night, I heard voices in the garden and could not sleep for fear I would wake up with a knife at my throat. When you died like that, slit from ear to ear, they called it the Algerian Smile.

One afternoon, through the light in the dining room door, I saw the outline of a figure: it was Bruno. He had flown to Algeria to work, and to be with me. He put his arms around me and held me against him. "I had to come anyway," he said. "So why not now? I got a visa."

He took me to a restaurant called El Djenina, like my

name. The owner knew him and hugged him hard, and Bruno, flirting, told me she was a remarkable woman. I felt jealous of this stranger, this Algerian woman in her sixties with white hair to whom he was paying so much attention. We went to my room, and I was startled to see he had brought his bag—he was planning on staying with me.

I was nervous so I put on my peach-coloured antique nightgown—bought on the Portobello Road by a friend for my birthday—in the bathroom and sat on the bed. He lay down next to me and rolled one lace sleeve down over my shoulder, then the other.

We did not, could not, sleep. We wandered through the rose garden. He wrote out all the words to the Jacques Brel song "Ne Me Quitte Pas," and we sat by the quiet pool at dawn as the birds began to call. The night-watchman passed us and asked Bruno for a cigarette. The scent of roses was overpowering. Sometimes we talked, sometimes we smoked and said nothing.

Sometime later we would arrive in Marseilles at dawn after travelling all night from Paris on the train. As we walked into the first bar we saw that was open for coffee, a man was sitting at the piano, still drunk from the night before. Several people hung on the bar, drinking cloudy glasses of Pernod and water, weary from their long night. We ordered Mauresque, the southern drink of almond syrup and Pernod, and as we sat down at a table, the drunk at the piano picked out with one finger Jacques Brel's "Ne Me Quitte Pas."

. . .

From that night in June when he stood in the doorway outlined in a pale light, many years and a dozen wars between us passed. There were endless phone calls, three miscarriages, much of what the French call *malentendu,* break-ups, a breakdown and a lot of alcohol. There was depression, death, suicides of friends, addiction and more times than I like to think when both of us nearly died.

There were several fallen cities, countless rebel armies and many times when Bruno said, "I want to be alone," and then tracked me down to Mogadishu or Grozny and said, "I can't lose you." There were times when I wanted to hide in a far corner of the earth to be away from him, and somehow he would always find me.

There were frenzied meetings in Dakar and Tora Bora, and an entire night in Jalalabad when we split up and I cried so hard that the photographer staying next door put his hand on my shoulder the next morning as I drank my coffee, bleary-eyed, before getting a car to Peshawar, and asked, "Are you all right?" Bruno and I did not speak after that time for a while. I had asked him, pointedly, to please leave me alone. Then I went to Africa to forget.

One night, in Somalia, after the tropical heat had died down, I climbed to the roof of the armed compound where I was staying to assemble my satellite phone. As I turned it on, amid the gunfire, the telephone rang. It was strange to hear the ring of a satellite telephone, to actually get an incoming phone call in the middle of Mogadishu. Whoever it was had awfully good timing.

It was Bruno, in Kigali Airport. He was in Rwanda on an

assignment. On the plane, looking down on the forests, he said he realized what he wanted. "Let's have a baby," he said. "Let's get married." I flew to Zimbabwe the week after that, and sometime later, after a few more wars, a few more skirmishes and a few close calls, we did.

CHAPTER 3

The Gun

The new, married, grown-up life in Paris was meant to be smaller, so we had both shed much of our past. Even so, Bruno's possessions, which were few, defined him. He was proud that he owned almost nothing but a motorcycle, the same one he had picked me up from the airport on and driven, at breakneck speed, to La Coupole. The few things he had brought back with him from his voyages around the world were like things looted from a pirate ship: as mystical and as unique as he was.

I did not know, and would not know for some time, what else he had brought back with him from Africa, but I knew about one thing he had left behind. It was his gun. He did not take it when he was packing up his life, closing up his life there, and for all I know it is still there, back in the huge, empty West African house that because of the conflict that would ravage that country no one would ever rent, as lovely as it was with its vast, cool garden of cocoa and mango trees, the swimming pool and the studio Bruno had painted apple green for me to write in.

He had left his gun behind, a magnum that I found under the bed in our villa in Abidjan, in the section of town named Cocody, on a street that had a number rather than a name, the second left near the Nuit de Saigon restaurant. I found it on a humid, wet morning.

Bruno had been posted to the Côte d'Ivoire, an African base from which he could report the entire continent. It was one day after the war had started, sometime in 2001. I was still sleepy, still in bed, but I leaned my head over the edge to try to find the flat red sandals I had kicked off the night before. There was only one, along with a pair of Bruno's dirty socks, but something else was gleaming on the polished white tile floor. And there it was: an enormous silver gun like something from *A Fistful of Dollars,* a movie I had watched over and over on Bosnian television many years before.

When I think of Africa, I see myself lying in bed in our room upstairs, behind the thick iron door, on top of pale green linen sheets. I had bought those sheets with Bruno on the rue St. Sulpice in Paris, at a shop called Maison de Famille; it was the first item we had ever bought together, after nearly a decade. I also see myself rising slowly in the heat—the sound of the birds squabbling noisily outside, the way they can only in Africa, a saraband of birds—and downstairs, I hear Bruno.

He's moving slowly with his morning ritual: the news in French; the BBC World Service tuned to Africa; the tea in an iron pot on a yellow-and-green plastic tray brought by Matthew, a refugee from Burkina Faso, and a peeled mango for me.

The country where we live is in a State of Emergency. It happened very quickly, the change from being a place of parties and barbecues and champagne receptions with tiny little finger sandwiches in the vast garden of the French Embassy to a place that smelled of death.

On the last night of normal life, Bruno and I went out to an Italian restaurant and ate veal and drank martinis to celebrate my finishing my book—I had gotten the internet to work that day, and I'd sent it off to my publisher.

The next day, Bruno left to go on an overnight trip, leaving me alone in the house with Alassane, the guard. I felt agitated, but Bruno reassured me.

"You'll be fine," he said. The country was so quiet, and news was so slow that he was going to make a film about French nuns who lived in the bush and made Camembert.

At night, I grew more wary, my childhood fears of the dark reflecting all the shadows in the room. I locked all the doors and turned out the lights and worked alone in the bedroom until very late. I was reading, I remember, a United Nations report on the genocide at Srebrenica. It disturbed me, and it was 3 a.m. when I finished. That was when I heard the shooting. I put down the report, turned out my light— I had learned that much from living in war zones before— and crawled to the window. In the sky were flares, shooting into the darkness like Fourth of July firecrackers. I could hear machine-gun fire somewhere further down the road, and the ominous sound of a Kalashnikov.

Not again, I thought. We came here to live in peace.

I was tired, but I knew I should not sleep. I crept back to bed and turned on my radio to the BBC World Service. There was nothing about Côte d'Ivoire. I picked up my cell phone, which had very little battery, and tried to call Bruno. A recorded message came on.

Then Alassane came running up the stairs, panting. "Madame, Madame, it's war! It's a war!" His eyes were wild. He had the key to the iron door that separated our bedroom from the rest of the house. He pushed me inside.

"Wait," I said. I ran down to the kitchen and grabbed a gallon of water, some bananas and my phone charger. From my study in the garden, I took my passport and my computer. I ran across the garden, my feet growing wet from the evening moisture, and back into my house. Up the stairs. Then Alassane shut the door and locked it. I could hear him running down the stairs. I was locked in, from the outside.

"Alassane!" I screamed. But he was gone.

We had no landline phone in the bedroom, and I estimated I had ten minutes' battery left on my cell phone. The electricity was going in and out. I phoned Fifi, the wife of another journalist who worked with Bruno. Fifi was languid and smart, Ethiopian by birth but educated at British boarding schools. She worked for UNICEF and was *branchée,* plugged in.

"What the FUCK is going on?"

"I have no idea," she said. She sounded calm. She had grown up as the daughter of a UN diplomat and had lived through the last round of violence in the Côte d'Ivoire. "It can't be another coup. Let me make some calls."

I sat on the edge of the bed for a moment, fully dressed, and then packed a small bag: passport, computer with my recently finished book on it, notebook, press cards.

Fifi phoned back thirty minutes later. "No one knows. Just lock yourself in, and don't go outside. Wait until the boys get back."

At 4 a.m., I heard the screech of tyres. A car was pulling into our drive. I heard someone running up the stairs. A soldier? *God, I hope not,* I thought. Then a pounding on the door, and then Alassane, I think, also coming upstairs, then someone opening the door.

It was Bruno. "Get your passport, get your things, and let's go."

"What's going on?"

"Come on, baby. No time. Just get in the car."

He didn't know either, I realized. Nobody did. I got in the back of the car. Eric, Fifi's husband, was driving. It was still dark, that time of night known as the hour of the wolf; the time, a doctor once told me, when most people died.

We took a shortcut through town and the hair stood on my neck. That intuition. That bad feeling.

"Don't go this way," I said suddenly.

No one listened to me.

I said it again: "I don't like this road."

I heard Eric and Bruno speaking rapid French. I could not understand them. Next to me was Sylvain, a young producer, crouched low in his seat.

A third time: "I don't like this road . . ."

"Tell your girlfriend to shut up," Eric said, annoyed. At that second, from the corner of my eye, I saw several young soldiers crossing the road in the filmy darkness, guns in their hands. They crept steadily across the road, as slowly as a caterpillar weaving across a pavement. They saw us and turned, guns forwards.

I slid under the seat, just as I heard the windshield crack from a bullet. Then another. Bruno had his camera in his lap and was filming. The glass shattered everywhere, and I heard him scream. A shard hit my arm.

"Are you hit? ARE YOU HIT?"

More bullets. Eric reversed fast, the wheels grinding into mud, and went backwards at high speed. I remember thinking: *Thank God a French guy is driving.* Sylvain and I crouched on the floor.

"I'm OK," Bruno shouted. His hand was bleeding. There was a cut on his face.

We got to the office of France Television in the centre of town, but no one knew what had happened. At 6 a.m., the phone rang. It was the foreign desk of CNN in London.

"What's going on down there?" someone shouted down the crackling line. "We are hearing news of a coup, we are hearing news of another war . . ."

I got on the phone and did a live report about not knowing what was going on, but describing the scenes in the street, the fear, the disorientation, the feeling in the air shortly before a country blows sky high.

The sun came up, full and hot. That was when we realised that the country was in a State of Emergency.

While Abidjan was falling to pieces, I was trying to get pregnant. The house near Nuit de Saigon was the only place we had lived together as a couple, and the only place that had any pretence of normalcy, any sense of a couple planning a future. We had a copy of a rental agreement with both our names on it. The bathroom was stocked with those sticks that tell you if you are pregnant or not and reserves of folic acid. By my bed was a copy of *What to Expect When You're Expecting*. Grown-ups.

But the coup and the violence stopped all that. The news said the same thing every day: updates of more territory the rebels had taken in the north, who had been killed the night before, which minister had replaced which. People burned out of their houses, people killed. This was exactly the kind of world that Bruno had told me, for years and years, that we could not bring a child into.

It was a morning like that when I found the gun. It lay on the clean white tiles like the reptiles I sometimes found in the house. But, unlike lizards, this was more repellent: huge, threatening. I pulled it out and lay it on my lap.

I have always been afraid of guns; I have seen so much of

what they can do. But they fascinate me too on some level: the power they have, the quickness of a bullet, the amount of time it takes to leave the barrel and reach someone's brain. Every country I ever worked in had some rebel army that carried Kalashnikovs, and I hate the sound of an AK-47. A photographer friend once told me it's only the bad guys, the non-conventional armies, that use them. If you hear one, you are already too close.

I never carried a gun and had only picked one up once before, in Central Bosnia as the city of Jajce was falling, and a soldier grabbed it abruptly out of my hand, telling me not to treat dangerous things like toys. I had been marched into the woods with a gun at my back in Kosovo, and once, in a cattle market in Africa littered with dead and wounded bodies, a soldier had pointed an AK-47 at my heart, the safety catch off.

And yet, and I did not know why, I was magnetically drawn to Bruno's gun. It was silver, like a little boy's imitation of a sheriff's gun. I weighed it in my lap. I ran my finger up and down the trigger, wondering what would happen if I pulled it. I even put it to my head to imagine what it felt like when people blew their brains out, as a friend of mine, another war reporter, had done shortly after he had said, "I've seen too much."

I put the gun back. I wondered if it was loaded, and assumed it was. Then I took a shower and dressed, pulling a lightweight cotton dress, made by Mr. Baa who had a shop around the corner, over my head.

Mr. Baa. I had given him one cotton dress and a width of

different coloured fabrics, and he had made me five African dresses. This one was a copy of a pink-and-black dress bought long ago in a boutique in Soho, and Mr. Baa had taken pride in covering the buttons with fabric and finishing the hem with hand stitching.

But I did not go to Mr. Baa any more, not since the day we drove to Bruno's office and I saw, in the empty field near Mr. Baa's shop, the naked corpse of a man with his hands bound by wire behind his back. A few days later, Mr. Baa took his son and his bolts of fabric and fled, north, I supposed. The country was now divided: north and south; Christian and Muslim.

Downstairs, the house was quiet. Bruno was on the patio, reading a two-day-old *Liberation* newspaper imported from France. I told him about the gun. He looked up with an unreadable expression. Then he looked down and kept reading the paper.

Matthew, the cook from Burkina Faso—the Burkinabe were being burned out of their homes and driven north—brought me coffee, tasting of acid, bitter, thin and weak, like all the coffee in the Ivory Coast. ("But how can a country that exports the most cacao in the world have bad coffee?" I would ask over and over, and no one would ever be able to answer.)

Matthew was small with a deeply scarred face from some tribal ritual. He was in his thirties, but looked ancient. He wore the same thing every day: baggy grey trousers, a freshly washed print shirt, and sandals, which he left by the back door when he came in. He padded through the house on wide, calloused feet that seemed to have no arch at all.

I liked Matthew because he seemed not to take life, which included his job, seriously. He dropped dishes and laughed. He burned the food and laughed. He dropped trays of coffee; broke the brand-new washing machine; shrank Bruno's trousers; dyed my white underwear navy blue and probably was responsible for the level of whisky in the bottle rapidly diminishing—though he blamed Alassane and Alassane blamed him.

The colonial French have never been good with domestic help, particularly in Africa, and Bruno often shouted at Matthew. I hated when he did, but Matthew did not seem to care. He laughed when Bruno raised his voice, laughed when Bruno left for work shrugging his shoulders in disbelief and laughed when I asked him about his many children.

One day, Matthew came to work late and said that his brother had died. He had been electrocuted from a wire that the families living in the shanty ran between shacks. We both stared at him.

"Go home, Matthew," Bruno said quietly. "You don't have to work today."

"You should be with your family," I said.

But Matthew did not want to go home. In Africa, he said, people died every day and it was as much a part of life as waking up in the morning. It just happened.

The day of his brother's death, Matthew washed up the breakfast dishes, and watered the plants, and did the laundry, padding up and down the cool stone stairs. He walked, as he did every day, to the market run by the little girl who had a withered leg from polio, who set up her shop on an old blanket in front of the video store, and came back with root vegetables to make a soup for lunch. I went back to my studio on the side of the garden to write. And I forgot, for the moment, about the gun.

Later on in the evening, we were eating more root soup covered with Gruyère cheese in deep bowls, and watching a video. We were lying on Mr. Baa's huge pillows, which he had made for the enormous living room. It was always hot downstairs, but upstairs Bruno turned on the air-conditioning until just before we went to sleep, to kill the mosquitoes. We were watching *Annie Hall,* and the shots of the Upper West Side seemed so foreign, like another planet, from the tropical heat, the languid trees of the Côte d'Ivoire.

I asked again about the gun. "Where did it come from?"

Bruno looked away. So much of him, I realized, I did not know, and would probably never know.

"But I don't understand . . . Why do you have it?"

"Forget about it." He picked up the remote for the video and paused the film.

"Who did you buy it from?"

"A man in the market." He turned to me. Anger darkened his face. "It's my business. Not yours. You don't own me." He turned the film back on.

The next day, he left for work. He turned to tell me what he'd told me every day since the *coup d'état* started in September: lock the door, don't let anyone in and don't wander around the streets. Remember the curfew and have a nice day. Try to find a flight to go home.

He added that last part because day by day, things were rapidly descending into chaos in Abidjan, government forces against rebel forces. How many wars had I reported that always came down to that? Government troops against a doctored up, rag-tail army, usually composed of kids.

But every day the fighting got heavier in the Côte d'Ivoire and the air began to smell like the air in Central Bosnia during the terrible days of ethnic cleansing. Gangs were burning people out of their homes, and raping women. We could smell the smoke from Cocody, and one morning we drove out to see a freshly burned-out house, and a family of refugees from Burkino weeping by the side of the smoldering ruins, their dishes broken, and a cooking pot at the father's feet.

What do you take with you when you run away? What do you take when you are driven from your house at gunpoint? How many times had I asked this question?

They always took what they could, what they could load on their shoulders, then they locked the door and ran away.

Bruno wanted me to go home. He did not like the risks I took when I worked, so he did not want me to work, though *The Times* and CNN phoned me daily, when they could get through, for updates. And, more, there was something he would not tell me, something he would never tell me, but I found out: he was in danger.

He did not feel comfortable working when I was alone at home. He worried about me. It was one thing to take responsibility for your own life, another to worry for someone else. He told me he could not concentrate, that my safety was a distraction for him. The curfews were earlier, the soldiers waiting at roadblocks more twitchy.

One night when I came back fifteen minutes after curfew from doing yoga with a friend in a nearby house, he was waiting outside, pacing. "Where were you?" he shouted. He saw my friend inside, and shouted to her: "This is not a game! They will shoot you for being out past curfew!"

My friend, who came from South America and was calm and clear, apologized. "We didn't realize it was this late."

"You didn't realize? Are you crazy? Do you know what's going on out there? It's not a joke!"

"I'm fine," I said. But for the first time, I sensed I was not really fine. I worked in my studio. I swam. I could not leave the house, but I wandered in the garden, picking the mangoes and coconuts. I counted my books on the shelf, and tried my cell phone, which still did not work. I went to the kitchen to help Matthew make the lunch soup: carrots, turnips and something dark and pungent and bitter which I had never seen before. I held up the ugly vegetable and shook it. "What is it?" But Matthew did not know its name. I suddenly felt lonely, isolated, strange.

One afternoon, in the north, we saw a truckload of men about to be taken away by government forces. The commander had gone, strangely enough, to Sandhurst and spoke some English. We sat with him in a garden, and he agreed to let me interview the prisoners.

I jumped in the back of the truck and one of them said, "Miss, please, take our names, our villages. They are going to kill us."

So while the government forces soldier stood outside the

truck, thinking I was interviewing them, I wrote, blinking back tears, all their names and villages, and their ages.

All that night, I tried phoning NGOs, trying to report the truck, the men and the incident. I finally reached someone on the overnight desk at the Red Cross. "We'll look into it."

Bruno said to me, with a touch of resigned cynicism: "They're probably in a mass grave already. You know that, don't you?"

But at night I kept dreaming of them, the way they grabbed my arm to write down their names, to tell their wives, their sisters, their mothers that they were on their way to death.

A few weeks later, Bruno came home at night in a dark mood. "I want you to leave."

"Because of the gun?"

"No, because of the war."

But it was because of the gun, or rather, what the gun represented. The real truth of the gun was this: if someone had come through the iron door that separated our bedroom from the other rooms in the house, Bruno would have used it. Sometimes I think because we were so close to the equator, so close to nature, so close to the smell of the earth, everything came faster—life, birth, illness, and then of course the inevitability of death. The terrifying thing was that neither one of us feared death enough.

We moved out of the house because it was no longer safe, to a hotel. I left everything but some dresses and my books. From the hotel, in downtown Abidjan, I had seen a crowd beat a Spanish tourist nearly to death simply because he was walking down the wrong street at the wrong time and they thought he was French. At this point, the French, the former colonials, were hated. I was watching from a window, drinking a can of Coke, and saw the crowd descend on the man.

"There's a man being beaten to death down there," I said to the three other reporters in the room with me who were frantically pacing, trying to get a phone line through to France. One French reporter came with me to the window and watched, but he said nothing. "Should we do something?" I said.

"Do what?" he said. "Call the police? The police are useless these days."

So we watched, helpless. The crowd got hold of the man's legs and his arms, and they pulled and pulled and beat him with sticks until some police managed to tear-gas the crowd and get to him.

I thought of the gun at my heart, the first day of the coup, when I tried to drag a wounded rebel into my taxi to take him to the hospital. The government soldier, young, probably scared, sweating, raised his gun to my chest.

A few weeks later, Bruno phoned a friend at the American Embassy as the evacuations of families and dependents, of NGOs and schoolchildren, missionaries and Peace Corps workers were going on. Planeloads of *les colons,* the colonials, headed back to countries they barely knew any more, leaving behind their big houses, their servants, their mango trees.

He put me on a flight to Paris. "It's better this way," he said.

"But I don't want to go."

It was late at night and he was driving to the north, to Bouake, to stay with the rebels, with a car full of other French journalists. I thought I might be pregnant, and without me knowing he had called the embassy and asked a friend to bump me up to the next flight out.

"You've got to go, baby," he said. "I can't work with you around."

In the headlights of the waiting car, with someone shouting out for him to hurry up, he kissed me goodbye. A *Paris Match* photographer snapped the picture of that moment, me tearful, him with his hands on my shoulders, leaning in to kiss me, determined, and there we are, our last night together in Abidjan. I was wearing Mr. Baa's polka-dot dress and sneakers.

"Please be careful," I said.

He smiled. Then he got in the car and drove away. The next day an armed escort from the American Embassy came to take me down the dangerous airport road—the first time in my career I ever had the luxury of any kind of protection—and I took the flight to Paris, tears of nerves and sorrow running down my face. The plane climbed higher in the clouds, and I watched the watery city of Abidjan below me fading from sight. I thought I saw the golden beaches of Grand-Bassam, where we had spent weekends walking; the shack where we ate barbecued chicken and drank beer before the war started; the long rows of roads fringed by bush.

I wasn't pregnant after all, but Bruno was right: it was time for me to go.

The plane was packed with families fleeing. Some of them were crying, and children roamed the aisles in a daze. We landed in Paris at five in the morning, and I waited to get a flight to London, my three suitcases containing my short life in Africa. It was the last time I would go to the Ivory Coast. But Bruno stayed on and on and on.

Have you ever been really scared?

All the time, I always say, because it is ridiculous to say otherwise.

But the truth is, I was not afraid when I was in the middle of chaos. It was real life with its vast responsibilities and wells of insecurities that frightened me.

In Sarajevo or Pristina or Baghdad or Abidjan, life was permanently on hold. Bills, pensions, marriage, divorce, loneliness, debt could not reach you in a bush or on a front line. You lived—like yogis holding a particularly difficult posture— only in the moment, because if you lost your concentration for that moment, you might lose your life or someone else's. You thought about your surroundings, you memorized what went by in the car you were driving, you concentrated on what people said.

War did not frighten me; cocktail parties in London, offices in New York and checking my bank account frightened me. The thought of my mother or my siblings dying frightened me. The gun in the white house in Cocody frightened me. It was something secretive that I did not know about Bruno. It was a place he did not want me to know, that perhaps he wanted to protect. It was separate, and darker than both of us.

CHAPTER 4

Moving to Paris

But now we were coming to live in Paris in the first week of a new year. We were refugees from the white house in Africa and there was a thirty-week-old baby in my belly. Since my departure from Abidjan, I had gone to Iraq, got married and fallen pregnant. Bruno had stayed on in the Côte d'Ivoire until the final weeks before the birth. We were reunited at Christmas 2003. The gun wasn't coming with us to Paris because Paris was a new life. Paris was taps with fresh water to take a bath, and electricity, and no flares in the sky scented with orange blossom, and telephones that worked, and doctors who had medicine to treat the wounded and sick.

We were coming to Paris as much for what it was as for what it wasn't. Paris was a northern European climate that did not make you feel like you always had a fever when you woke in the morning. There were no car bombs or road checks or crazed ten-year-old soldiers waving RPGs in your face. Paris was not going to be mothers from Russia or Chechnya or Srebrenica crying that their sons had never come home while I scribbled in my notebook, trying not to cry with them. Paris would not be mass graves in Kosovo, and Sierra Leonean children whose arms had been amputated, deliberately, above the elbow or above the wrist to give them "long sleeves or short sleeves" by insane rebels fighting a war no one understood.

More than this, we were coming to Paris because I was going to have a baby and I was in my fourth decade of life, the past two of them spent wandering the earth. And I wanted, I *needed*, to be stable, to wake up and know where I would be that day, that night, the next morning. I wanted to wake up next to Bruno and know that he would not be taken away from me by Africa, by Kosovo, by tsunamis in Asia or hurricanes in America.

Our apartment was on a narrow street that started at the Tuileries, the gardens where the children of Marie Antoinette once played; they say it was one of the last beautiful things that the queen saw as she was being driven to prison. At the end of the Tuileries was the Place de la Concorde, where she would be beheaded. There is sometimes a Ferris wheel there now, and once or twice, Bruno would take me up on it. From the top you could see all of Paris: the hills of Montmartre and the dome of Sacré Coeur, the Montparnasse Tower, the winding streets near the Sentier, and further out, the flatness leading to eastern Paris and Bercy. I could also, if I squinted, see the roof of our building, 5, rue du 29 Juillet. On the northern side, our street ran into rue Saint-Honoré, and then a bit further on there was a square with a market. Three times a week vendors sold vegetables, flowers, potted geraniums in season, Christmas trees, handmade embroidered nightgowns from Madagascar, salt from the Ile de Ré, and a few stalls with food from Napoli that was as familiar to me as my own name: the food of my childhood, from my grandfather's house, and his long, long mahogany table. There were piles of de Cecco pasta, little hard Italian biscuits, roasted peppers, aubergine rolled with ricotta, slices of prosciutto laid out in intricate patterns behind glass and, lined up in a triangle, jars of Brioschi, a lemon-flavoured stomach medicine that fizzled in a glass of water, which my father used to take when I was a child.

Our street was named after a law passed in 1881, which protected the freedom of the press and the right to hang posters on city monuments. Occasionally, I would see it scrawled for no reason at all on walls in other parts of the city—*Loi de 29 Juillet*—like a freedom cry. It was to be our first real home together outside of a war zone.

And our home in Paris was a beautiful place. The first time I saw it, I was let in by a cleaning lady who thrust open the heavy door and proudly showed me inside. There were huge great rooms with high ceilings full of light that poured onto the parquet floors, and corridors that led to room after room. I walked through, the cleaning lady following me, wondering how lucky I had been.

"Your lucky star again," Bruno said when I phoned him

in Abidjan later to tell him, as I stood on the balcony. But I had worked hard to get the owner to rent it—it was owned by a young Italian artist who did not particularly want to give it up, had no need to, and besides, the place was stuffed with easels and paints and enormous canvasses that he did not want to remove. If he had wanted to, he could have rented it for much more than I could pay.

I had met O. at an English christening in Somerset, on a scorching July day, and I tried to convince him, even though I had never seen it, that we had to have this apartment. I did not know the neighbourhood—the Right Bank and the Tuileries were not places I would have gone often—and he tried to tell me, gently, that it was perhaps too big for us, code for too expensive. But I was pregnant, we were getting married in a month, and Bruno was still in Africa. The job of finding our home had been given to me.

It was the middle of the European heat wave, when people were dying in the scorching temperatures, old people could not breathe, and we got warnings to stay indoors. During that English countryside lunch, most of the guests got up and stripped off their clothes and swam in the river, and I sat balancing my salad and trying to convince O. to lend me his flat. By the end, O.—still uncertain—scribbled down instructions on how to find the apartment, the code to the front door that led to the courtyard and where to find the cleaning lady who would let me in.

A few weeks later, with the taste of iron in my mouth from early pregnancy, and fighting morning sickness with a bag of ginger sweets, I took a very early train from Waterloo

Station. By the time I arrived in Paris Gare du Nord, feeling utterly sickened by the suffocating heat, there was a long row of people waiting for cabs. I did not then know that in France, if you are pregnant or have children you can go to the head of the line and no one complains. I waited, and took a cab to the address O. had written down.

The driver wove down Boulevard de Magenta through the grimy streets of the 10th arrondissement with the Turkish bars, then the 9th, past old theatres and nightclubs from the 1950s, past airline offices from obscure countries (I noticed a sign for Air Ivoire and flinched) and old-fashioned dance hall restaurants. He passed the Grands Boulevards, on to the rue Sainte-Anne with all the Japanese noodle bars, turned into the lovely, leafy area of Palais-Royal where I would later take my son and sit under chestnut trees to happily breastfeed him. He took me down rue de Richelieu, left on rue Saint-Honoré and deposited me on the corner of my street, pointing out that it was a one-way.

There was an intimidating trendy boutique called Colette on the corner, with a gaggle of Japanese tourists and a man inside the window dressing a naked mannequin. There was a patisserie across from that, and the smell of almond cakes. There was a church with stone stairs leading to the entrance, St. Roch, which Napoleon once shelled with canons, where our son would be baptized, and where I would push him nearly every day as an infant in his stroller to light a candle. And where, my mother-in-law told me, the wife of Louis XIV prayed and prayed for a child, and when her child was born, he was held in front of the baptismal font, which is why every child who is baptized there, mine included, is held up to the font.

There was a café where a few people sat drinking Coca-Cola and fanning themselves in the heat. There was a friendly pharmacy, a clothes shop and an optician. It was, as Bruno would later say, a working neighbourhood. This was to be my new quartier, my new home.

In London, my street smelled like nothing. In the spring, there was sometimes the faint fragrance of blossom when the dogwood trees outside were in bloom, but usually there was just the flat metallic smell of the rain. My first street in Paris smelled of yeast: of baking bread, of cakes. That morning, and nearly every morning for the three years we lived there, there was the same smell, which hit me as soon as I reached the green door that was the entrance of our courtyard: warm, half-baked bread. Every morning it was like this, except in January, right before the baby came. During that time, when I was at my most enormous and most desperate to get a good night's sleep, it smelled of almond paste from the galette des rois, the cake that is eaten for the Epiphany, the feast of the three kings.

The feast is traditionally celebrated after Christmas, in a time I have always associated with the Orthodox Christmas celebrated in Sarajevo with gunfire. Holidays and springtime traditionally heat up war: offensives are usually in the spring, and my calendar had been determined by battles and front lines. But now, it was about holidays and turning seasons and the smells in the street. The January tradition in France, in my new war-less life, was this: on that day, when the three kings brought gold, frankincense and myrrh to the newborn baby Jesus, the French father brings home a round golden cake baked with warm almond paste.

The family gathers round the table, and the youngest child hides underneath it. He gets to point to which slice of galette goes to which member of the party. Inside one piece of cake is a small ceramic toy, and whoever bites into it gets to wear the paper crown and choose a beautiful queen. When I am impatient now, when I want something to happen quickly, I think of the taste of almond paste in my mouth. Because those days and weeks before my son came, when I would eat the galette des rois for breakfast, were also about impatience, but twinned with the sense of wonder. I was anticipating something fearsome and ferociously wonderful that was going to come into my life.

But even in summer, even before I reached this crucial time of waiting and almond cake, even while the baby was the size of an apple seed, rue du 29 Juillet smelled of baking bread. It made me feel warm; it made me feel—for the first time since I left for Sarajevo in 1992 and realized that everything evil can and will happen—that perhaps everything would be all right.

I punched in the code to the green door, which was impossibly heavy, walked into a cobbled courtyard littered with light, a row of jasmine plants against one wall, and took the lift to the fifth floor.

O. had arranged for the cleaner to meet me, and she was there on time, a French working-class woman with a sweet nature. She waved away her hand when I apologized for being late. But even before she pulled the heavy keys from her pocket and opened the double green doors that led to the flat, I had the feeling I get when I know something will effortlessly work. *This is going to be our home,* I thought, *where my baby will be born, and where we will always be happy.*

Inside, the flat was darkened against the canicule, the killer heat wave that was by now decimating France, but I could see the largesse of the rooms, the hauteur, the parquet floors, the light streaming from a small glass room that led off the kitchen, where a few straggly plants were dying in the heat.

The artist had not lived here for some time, and it had the smell of a place that had been shuttered closed. It was not clean, and there was too much grand, dark furniture cluttering the space. It looked like an elegant flea market: there were three or four enormous nineteenth-century sofas in one room, a dark wood dining room table squashed by a chaise longue, paintings, easels, books, the smell of paint and paint thinner, piles of old magazines, marble tables, a pointy obelisk that looked frighteningly dangerous, and a long, canary yellow sofa that looked like it came from 1970s Sweden.

The cleaner opened one of the shutters to a door that opened onto a balcony. It ran the entire length of the apartment. I stood outside the bedroom balcony, next to a withered grapevine, and saw, across the Tuileries, the clock on the top of the Musée d'Orsay.

The cleaner said, "It's a big apartment. For Paris."

There was a long, narrow hallway stuffed with yet more

sofas and paintings; a bedroom painted dark maroon; another room—the baby's room, I decided—with a wooden bed from Kerala in Southern India. The master bathroom had an old-fashioned claw-foot tub. There was an office with a balcony and a fireplace for me to work, and a large dining room for friends to gather and eat. The kitchen was painted apple green, like my study in Africa.

There were jars of pasta, and heavy iron pots hanging from silver hooks. There were salt shakers and thick dishes from Sicily. It felt, I thought, like a country house in Tuscany. I thanked the cleaner, handed back the key and left.

In the Place du Marché Saint-Honoré, I found a café with long, scrubbed wooden tables, and I ordered a tea and a lemon tart and called O. from my cell phone. I am not sure who convinced whom, or what arrangements were made, or how he was eventually convinced, but in the end, I called Bruno and told him we had a home for our family.

The taxi driver who picked me up on the corner of rue de Rivoli to take me back to Gare du Nord came from Uganda. He spoke English. I told him I had lived and worked in Africa.

"Then you know," he said. He did not have to say what I knew.

"What do you miss about Africa?" I said. I told him I missed the air right before the rainy season, when it was perfectly still, and then the rains came, and the time of morning when the light was still pink, just after dawn, when you saw everyone on the road walking to work. I thought briefly of Matthew, our cook in Abidjan, walking to work on the day his brother died. In Africa, people walk slowly, with great patience, but always with a destination.

We were stuck in traffic for a long time. I could see the Gare du Nord from where we sat, in front of an Egyptian café where a group of men sat reading Arabic newspapers and drinking tea and smoking water pipes.

I once had a friend from Zimbabwe, a writer called Shimmer. We were meant to meet for lunch in a café in midtown Manhattan one afternoon and he was late. When he arrived, he drank a large glass of water and told me he had spent the morning walking the length of Manhattan Island. "It reminded me of being home," he said.

"You *walked* the entire island?"

"Yes, walked. Is that so strange?"

Later, Shimmer told me, "You can always tell someone who is very far from the place of their birth by the sadness in their eyes."

"I miss the moon," the driver said finally when he dropped me off. "That's what I miss the most about Africa."

On the train, I thought about how I had spent most of my life missing something. When I left for England from America when I was very young to go to school, I missed my family. When I was working in strange places, with long days and no sleep, I missed laughter, I missed the normality of daily life and routines, and I missed faces whose features I knew and could feel safe near.

I already knew that I was going to miss London, the city, and the life I had before: the people in the cafés, the greyness of a November day, the newsagents and the Sunday papers, and the smell of roasted, slightly burnt potatoes on Portobello Road. My gypsy life. But I also knew that I was going to have a happy life in that dirty, cluttered, and over-furnished Right Bank apartment.

That was the summer, and the apartment did not become ours until the new year. As my body grew, people told me my life was going to change. This surprised me. They said it in a conspiratorial way, as if this would be a terrible thing. They did not know, I suppose, how desperately I wanted my life to change.

I did not want to wake up in a bed in Africa with a gun underneath it. I did not want to crawl to windows in the dark to see which direction the shooting was coming from. I did not want to hide underneath car seats to avoid getting hit by stray bullets. I was sick of bribing corrupt officials, begging for visas at outpost embassies, hiring interpreters, landing in a place where no one knew me, and piling chairs against the doors of filthy, remote boarding houses, drugging myself with codeine so that I could sleep, terrified someone would rob or rape me.

I was tired of my maps, my notebooks, my penknives, my flashlights, my compass, and my spare batteries, my BBC World Service. I hated my wardrobe of khaki trousers and desert boots and linen shirts and sneakers. Or the winter things: thick padded coats, Gore-Tex boots for climbing over snow-crested mountains to countries I was not supposed to be in.

September passed, October and November. I was aware, for the first time in many years, of seasons changing and being present while they did, not being on planes going into different climates and time zones. As my baby grew, Bruno stayed in Africa to work, throughout the rainy season, and the war in the Ivory Coast grew more and more violent.

But he told me nothing when he phoned every morning and every evening; he protected me from the bullets, the fires, the beatings, the abuse he was taking. He did not tell me that he locked himself in every night and drank to stop the fear from creeping inside. He did not tell me that everyone had run away, that he and his crew were practically the only journalists who had not fled. Fifi, my Ethiopian friend, had left with her small daughter. Most of the NGOs we knew had closed down.

All through that autumn, when the leaves shook down from the trees in front of my London flat, grey against the wet streets, and I planted purple heather in my window boxes for the last time, I took care of myself and the baby. But the more I read about childbirth and babies, the more I began to feel an emotion I had discarded long ago on all of those long rides through Liberian jungles and Bosnian mountains: fear.

It seemed likely, according to my books, that so much could go wrong at any second. I worried about the baby being born dead, or losing him weeks before he arrived. I worried that when I went for scans, there would be no heartbeat, and I would see again the startled look on the technician's face as they had to tell me the baby was no longer there. I worried about the contaminated air I had breathed in Iraq for so long. I worried about birth defects.

But the question I could not ask the doctor who took care of me—English, competent, remote—was the one that tormented me the most: Could I do this? Had I been too damaged, had I seen too much, walked through too much, lived too much, to give this baby good things? How could I ever show him the world was a beautiful place when I was not sure I believed it myself?

The doctor examined me every few weeks, bemused and slightly impatient at my strange questions. He answered them in a straightforward but not particularly enthusiastic manner, one by one, dispassionately dealt with.

I went for all my tests. The technicians rubbed gel on my belly and made jokes, but I was frantic until I could see the baby's heartbeat on the screen.

"Is he dead?" I asked, and they would turn to me, frowning, uncertain.

"Why would you say that? Here's his heart. Here is his beautiful little face."

The day I found out Luca was a boy—I had assumed, as had Bruno, that he would be a girl—I phoned Bruno in Abidjan and told him. There was a pause, the usual crackle of the terrible phone lines connecting us from London to Africa. Then he burst into tears.

And so, perhaps in denial of my new role, and unsure of my identity, as the autumn grew colder, I went to Palestine, in the middle of the second intifada, to work.

I landed at Ben Gurion Airport and took an early morning taxi to Jerusalem, the car climbing higher and higher into the city which had meant so much to me in my former life—my first big story, the first time I walked into the American Colony Hotel in the late 1980s and saw a gaggle of foreign correspondents gathered around a Reuters machine spurting out wire copy and realized I wanted to be part of it.

My very first trip was the beginning of the first Palestinian intifada, and it was the first time I saw a refugee camp, or met someone who had been brutally tortured and survived. It was the first time I went to the Gaza Strip, and heard gunfire. It was the first time I experienced a checkpoint, soldiers pointing guns, and adolescent fighters, their faces covered in *keffiyehs,* hurling stones at windscreens.

I met teenagers who were on the run from the law, for whom I waited anxiously in safe houses; mothers of Jewish soldiers who had been killed serving in the territories; a Palestinian mayor who had lost both his legs in a car-bomb attack; and a woman who would change my life forever: an Israeli lawyer defending Palestinians in military court. She told me to go everywhere, write everything, and gave me a brief, a blueprint for life: if you have the chance to give a voice to people who do not have a voice, she told me in her decrepit office in West Jerusalem, then you have an obligation.

I was only in my mid-twenties and I took her words very seriously. I was so young that I remember being embarrassed by my youth, by my inexperience, by my lack of nerves—those would come later—when a veteran correspondent bought me a drink and said, "How old are you, anyway?" And when I answered, embarrassed, rounding off my age to my next birthday, he laughed and looked even more perplexed.

Now I was returning, pregnant, much older, and this second intifada was even more violent, even more tragic than the first. There were more settlements in East Jerusalem and the West Bank since my last trip back just a year before, and the children I had spent years interviewing in Gaza and Ramallah and Jenin and Nablus were grown up, some dead, some in jail, some in exile. The man who had stood in Gaza with me during my first trip and told me he imagined peace sometime in the next fifteen years was long gone. The tactic used by Palestinians, who felt they had nothing to lose, was to employ their young as suicide bombers. Everything and nothing had changed.

The light on the ancient stone walls in West Jerusalem was turning pink the morning I arrived, the same way it had on that first journey all those years ago, and I could see people rushing to work: the men in their long coats and side curls and beards and nineteenth-century hats, the women in scarves and long dresses, the tiny children, everyone moving rapidly towards something. I saw the fierceness of the pink of the bougainvillea that grows against the stone walls. The grey hill towns, the light on stone. I counted back the events of my life and my visits to Jerusalem.

I remembered once arriving a few days after my father's funeral. I was still numb. Yitzhak Rabin had just been murdered and my office had phoned me in the middle of the night, as soon as the news broke. I took an early flight from Heathrow, packing one of my father's cotton dress shirts, which I had stolen from his drawer the day after the funeral. It still had his smell. At night, in my hotel room in Jerusalem, I slept in it, and one morning I went to the Mount of Olives and left a piece of paper with his name.

Another afternoon, rainy and cold, the skies open and menacing, I took a taxi to Bethlehem, passing through the ancient stony hills, past the shepherds who looked as though they could be in a tableau a thousand years old. I went to the Church of the Nativity, and left another paper with his name. "You are there. You are always with me," I said out loud to no one; schoolchildren and pilgrims gathered around me.

This trip to Israel, now that I was pregnant, would be different, more cautious. Bizarrely, the doctor was not concerned about buses being blown up by suicide bombers; he had said it was all right for me to come, as long as I was careful about what I ate.

"Well, the food's fine there, isn't it?" he said cryptically. I thought it was the strangest question. Because as it turned out, I could not eat much. I sat in the bar of the American Colony, where I had sat on and off for the past two decades, and ate roast beef sandwiches and drank Coca-Cola, and then got ill. The barman, who had known me since I had started coming to the hotel, made jokes about the time when another journalist and I swam naked late one night in the pool. That wasn't me, I said, and in fact, it seemed like it was not me at all—someone else living my life through me, perhaps.

At 8 p.m. most nights I went to bed. I was sick in the

night and sick when I woke up in the morning. Something felt wrong, and I phoned my mother in America. "I'm sick all the time," I told her.

"Honey," she said patiently, "I had morning sickness for nine months with all seven of my children."

In the early morning, I went to refugee camps with my driver to seek out stories about suicide bombers, but the dust made me cough. Six months earlier, a doctor in New York had discovered that I have a rare blood-clotting disorder—two, in fact; a condition so rare that she asked permission to teach her students about it—and told me that throughout my pregnancy I should take injections of blood thinner to prevent a miscarriage.

I had lost three babies before this baby, and I was determined not to go through that again—the trauma of a profound loss—and I would have given myself ten needles a day if I had to. This baby, this one inside me, made with the man I loved more than anything in the world, was hard-won, and I would do everything to keep him. Every morning I sat on the bed, clenching my teeth in fearful anticipation of the sting as I slid the needle under the skin of my thighs and belly, trying to find a spot that was not bruised.

Worse, though, was the larger intramuscular needle—this one full of progesterone, which allegedly would keep the baby inside me—which hurt. I could not reach the spot on my back where I needed to inject it, so I had to enlist friends or whoever was near me at the time to give it. I rated my friends on a scale of how skillful they were at piercing my skin. "Just throw it like a dart," I told them, wincing.

Some were good and some were bad. Some hit nerves that made me jump. *I am doing this for someone else,* I thought. *I am doing this for my baby.* My friend hovered above me in the bathroom of a Japanese restaurant holding the enormous syringe in her hand, squeezing out the air bubbles; she was so nervous her hand shook.

"Fuck, I can't do this."

"Yes you can," I coached. "And more to the point, you have to."

She stood back, shut her eyes, and jabbed.

The mothers of the suicide bombers and the potential suicide bombers, women my age who had given birth ten or eleven or twelve times, told me something was wrong. They brought me cup after cup of mint tea, heavily sugared, and made me lie down on their dusty cushions. They would lay their hands on my stomach and tell me the baby was strong, but their faces looked worried.

When I walked through the markets I had once loved, in the Old City or in Salahadin Street, everything smelled stronger, more intense, sharper, and it made me sicker. I could smell the cardamom in the coffee and the raw meat hanging in the halal meat stalls. I sat in the back of a taxi on the way to East Jerusalem, and breathed the aroma of old cigarettes, and asked the driver to go slower; sometimes we stopped near olive groves and I got out and sat until the waves of sickness passed.

Bruno called me again and again from Africa: from demonstrations, from the north of the country where he was living with rebels, from his office in the centre of Abidjan where I had filed my copy the first night of the coup. I missed him profoundly, and the sense of protection I always felt when he was near. At night, I dreamed of him, sometimes in peril, sometimes at peace.

"Everything," he told me, "is going to be all right." No one in my entire life had ever told me that. And I believed him.

I came back to my room and lay on my bed watching CNN and writing up my notes about the logic behind becoming a suicide bomber. When I walked to the bar, the Palestinian cleaning lady, who had known me since I was twenty-five, stopped me. She shook her head. She asked how I was sleeping. "You look sick," she said. "Not radiant, like a pregnant woman."

One night, I began to bleed and bleed, and I took a taxi to the hospital with a friend. I remember walking through the sliding doors and making a deal with God: *Please don't let me have another miscarriage. If I can have this baby, I will offer you anything: my own health, my job, even love. Just please let this baby be born alive.*

I was back where I had been so many nights over the past two years, since Bruno and I decided to become parents. But this time Bruno wasn't with me. Another hospital, another dressing gown that opened in the back, another pair of stirrups and another ultrasound. And now, another language: Hebrew.

The doctor arrived. He was Orthodox, had a strong Brooklyn accent and was efficient and pleasant. "Can I ask you a personal question?" he said, moving the cold ultrasound wand over my skin. "Do you want this baby? I mean really want this baby?"

"Yes, of course I want this baby."

"Well," he said. "You are certainly not acting like some-one who wants a baby. You're dilating, but it's much too early for the baby to come, and you're wandering around the West Bank. If I were you, I would go to your hotel, get into bed and stay there. Until the due date."

It shocked me, his frank judgement. I went to another doctor at a different hospital, this one closer to Tel Aviv. This doctor was famous for operating on women with ovarian cancer, and he was older, softer. He examined me and took my elbow to help me slide off the table. He sat behind his desk and looked at my records. He told me I needed surgery, and that I should fly home to England to have it. "I could do it," he said gently. "But I think you want to be with your husband."

"My husband is in Africa," I said, and suddenly felt very alone. My throat tightened.

"You'll be fine," the doctor said in a fatherly tone. "Go home. Have the surgery and then stay in bed. You are going to be just fine."

I went back to the hotel and packed my bag, twisting my computer cables and folding my maternity dresses while Alex, the Italian photographer I worked with for years, watched me, smiling. He was the only person Bruno trusted me with when we were on assignment. "Pass the phone to Alex," he would say when Alex and I were together in Iraq or Afghanistan, Gaza or Kosovo.

I would hear Bruno talking. And I would hear Alex say: "I will, man."

"What did he say?" I would ask Alex, and he would laugh. "Always the same thing: Take care of her."

I went home to London and had the operation. Bruno was stuck in the Ivory Coast, but he phoned every hour. Endurance, I kept thinking, have endurance. I stayed in bed until the snow came, until Christmas, and then Bruno came back, and we packed up my little flat, and I gave away most of my books and clothes because I wanted to make a fresh start, and we went forwards, to Paris, together.

CHAPTER 5

Settling Down into Pregnancy

Most women prepare endlessly for their first child; but I have prepared assignments with more attention. For this, my biggest assignment, I was lost, and torn with superstition. If I prepared too much, what if God destroyed my brittle happiness?

It was not a smooth pregnancy. Every bloodstain, every pull in my abdomen, every cough was a trip to the emergency room in panic: another scan, or nights in the hospital linked up to electronic devices. I spent weeks in an isolation unit while doctors checked me for TB and whooping cough or some infectious disease that lingered in my system from years on the road. The past, one of the doctors said to me, remains in the body's memory.

I did not have a layette—I was too superstitious to buy

baby clothes because of the past miscarriages—the only article of clothing I had was a tiny pair of mittens from Guatemala that I had bought years ago, thinking that someday I might have a child.

I did not do yoga, have a birth plan, or even have a firm due date—when the doctor talked to me, it was only to plan as far as the next visit: "Let's see how we go," he said. "You're probably going to deliver early." I was doomed to remain in the present, unable to plan for the future.

At night, I had vivid dreams, nightmares sometimes, of Africa, or the Balkans. All of the things that had never frightened me before—pain, for instance—were slowly creeping into my life like a patient waking up from anaesthetic.

A friend brought over a pile of used maternity clothes for me to borrow. "Have you bought a crib? And a car seat?" she asked, looking around my flat. "Don't you even have a blanket to wrap the baby in when you come out of the hospital?" She burst out laughing. "You're in denial! You're going to be a mother! It still has not sunk in, has it?"

But I was not in denial—I was in shock. Some women know all their lives they will have children. I loved children, loved how they smelled, loved the things they said, loved the way they moved and their clothes and haircuts, and their books and music boxes. But I remembered my childhood as something distant, slightly painful and lonely.

Every time I thought about it, something told me I was not ready. Even as my friend Gillian gave me a baby shower, and all my girlfriends arrived with blue packages and tiny sweaters and onesies—how could I ever fit a baby's arm inside a onesie without breaking it?—and a special bucket for diapers, and a blue winter coat with adorable toggles, I sat in my chair, smiling and filled with gratitude and love for my friends, all the time wondering what the hell I was doing.

My own mother, my sister and nearly all the women in my family had full-time jobs as mothers. They were wonderful at it. They drove their children back and forth to soccer, skating lessons, piano lessons, private schools, but I sensed, even in my own mother, a kind of distant dissatisfaction.

Every time I went to the doctor when I was in my twenties, he repeated the same thing to me: don't wait too long to have children. But since then I had spent nearly two decades seeing children wrecked and traumatized by war. I saw babies born in the middle of a siege, saw amputated limbs, kids who stepped on landmines, a young swimmer who lost her breast to shrapnel, budding nine-year-old soccer players who lost their hands to American smart bombs, kids who had breakdowns, kids who were blown up by mortars as they were building snowmen.

I saw kids orphaned from AIDS in Africa and India, and I held them and fantasized about bringing them away with me and giving them a home and food and real medical treatment, but the fact was, I was not entirely sure I—who could barely take care of myself unless it was in the midst of chaos—could care for them. And seeing all of that, as much as I protested that it had done nothing to me, alienated me from people who had never seen it at all. When I returned to

London from my assignments, the only people I wanted to see were people I did not have to explain anything to, people who did not ask questions, people who had seen what I had seen. And Bruno, who knew me, who understood me and who spoke a language identical to mine.

I played Russian roulette with my biological clock, and then when the time came and I felt capable of becoming a mother, it was almost too late. I got pregnant very easily. But the weeks would pass, I would buy special oil to rub on my belly for stretch marks, and maternity dresses, and then one night I would wake up in agonizing pain and get rushed to the hospital, and a grim-faced nurse or doctor would tell me the baby was dead.

No one could work out what was happening, why my body kept failing me, and I spent what seemed like months inside the labs of St. Mary's Hospital, Paddington, having blood test after blood test. Finally, someone, a doctor in New York worked it out: my niece and my mother suffered from a rare blood-clotting disorder, and one day, I found out I had the same thing. But it took years to discover, and years for this baby to come down to earth.

In the Bible, both Sarah and Rachel, who had very late and very yearned-for babies, are told that the child who is much desired, much waited for, is always special. And I had waited so very long for my Luca.

When I finally held him firmly inside me, I tried to act appropriately: I thumbed through my copy of *What to Expect When You're Expecting,* but I only got through the first chapter. Nothing in it seemed to relate to me. Someone loaned me a Moses basket with long handles so I could carry the baby everywhere, which was my plan. When people asked what I would do about work, I would shrug and say I would take the baby with me in the basket. In truth, I had no clue what I would do or how I would manage my life.

When my boss, a man with many children, found out I was pregnant, he brought me into a small office, his face full of anger. "I've got a war correspondent who can't go to war," he said.

"I'm allowed to get pregnant, aren't I?" I responded, but he talked about contracts, and Iraq, and maternity leave and getting back to work, and I knew then that I could never do it again, not the way I had before. I knew that I would miss reporting the war that was breaking out in Baghdad, in Basra, in Mosul, but I realized for the first time I had made a choice, and that I had to stand by it.

He finally stopped talking, still angry, and I sat in my chair, slightly dazed. I'm not sure I knew then how deeply the addictions of being in those places, those times, watching countries fall apart and being put back together again, had affected me.

In my London flat with the crooked wooden floors and the windows that did not shut firmly, I lay on the bed and talked to the baby, just like every other mother-to-be. I told him everything: about his father, who was far away in Africa, about the mango tree and the green studio where I wrote, about how we met, about our wedding in the Alps during the heat wave, about how the entire wedding party had trooped through the wheat fields, past the barns, to visit the statue of Our Lady and lay flowers at her feet. I asked him to come out healthy and strong and brave.

On a couple of occasions, before she died at the age of ninety, I met Martha Gellhorn, the third wife of Hemingway, and a war correspondent herself.

The first time I met her, in the early 1990s at the start of the war in the former Yugoslavia, she was remote. Mutual friends had warned me she was difficult: she was tricky, she did not like other women, but somehow I had convinced myself that when we met, it would be different. Above all, her friends whispered, do not mention Ernest Hemingway.

For our first meeting, I was going to interview Gellhorn for a reissue of a collection of her war reporting, and it took me all day to get from London to her remote cottage in Wales. I took trains, buses and finally a taxi, which dumped me at the edge of a field. I hiked in the blazing sun, and wondered what I would say to this woman who I was hoping would be my mentor, would tell me things about how to live my life and where to go and who to meet.

I was twenty-eight years old, and had recently left my first husband, a photographer I had met at university. I was free. I wanted her to advise me how to be an independent woman, how to work in a man's world, how to report real issues, how not to be afraid. I had felt the same way when I met the legendary Vietnam War reporter Gloria Emerson at her home in Princeton, and she had been equally distant. Both of them were powerful writers who understood chaos and destruction and death, but both were notoriously difficult in real life, had complicated love lives, and neither had ever given birth. Was it war that had done this to them, had somehow frozen them in time away from real life?

Gellhorn, who Hemingway once described as "grace under pressure," opened the door, elegant and beautiful in slim trousers, a neat blouse, and a burning cigarette. She was as lovely looking as Lauren Bacall. "Don't think you're getting lunch," she said a bit fiercely, "because you're not." Instead, because it was hot, she gave me a glass of iced water. Later on, she did show me her upstairs bathroom, and she had laid out a fresh towel for me, so perhaps she was not as thoughtless as she was trying to appear. In the end, we talked for many hours. She called me "my dear girl"—I must have seemed very young to her—and although I longed for one of her slender cigarettes, I did not have the courage to ask. We watched television together. The war in Slovenia had just started, and she made historical references to Yugoslavia that I did not yet understand.

Nothing ever happens to the brave—that is what they said about her, and that day I realized above all what she had: courage. I wanted a life like hers, courageous, free and unencumbered.

I met her one more time. A few years had passed, and now I was what they called a war reporter, although I could never say it without great embarrassment, because it was not what we—the tribe I worked with, who travelled round and round the world from conflict to conflict—called ourselves. It was something other people called us. I was older, and we were on a panel together about the ethics of reporting. Although I had agreed to sit on the panel, I had done so with trepidation—after my article on Gellhorn had appeared several years back, she had written me a letter in a neat, spidery handwriting on pale blue paper with MARTHA GELLHORN embossed at the top. She hated the article. She called me a liar for describing her cottage as "light filled." She said it was not full of furniture as I had described—she counted the pieces and listed them. She said I had committed the cardinal sin against journalism—lying. And worst of all, I had mentioned Hemingway when I had promised her publicist I would absolutely not. Hemingway had treated her terribly during their marriage. He had cheated on her, stolen her stories and her contacts, humiliated her, and her life after him was spent trying to live down the shadow of being the third Mrs. Hemingway. My editor had insisted I mention him at some point, and I did not fight it enough. In those days, I was very intimidated by editors.

But I was more intimidated by Martha Gellhorn. I cried and cried when I got the letter. By then, I had another kind man in my life. He made me a cup of tea and rubbed my arm and told me, "Darling, don't worry about it—she was probably having a bad day." But I did worry. I put the letter in a wooden box high on my shelf, and it stayed there, a burning shame then, and sometimes even now it hurts.

And so, with this letter in mind, I faced her. In fact, I sat next to her on the panel, and we were photographed together. Somewhere that photograph still exists. She greeted me warmly and kissed me on both cheeks. The meeting in Wales a decade earlier seemed to have been forgotten. Martha was very old but still very beautiful. She was draped in scarves, tall, slender, with snowy hair and exquisite bone structure.

She called me "dear girl" again.

Martha died when she was ninety. It was whispered, but never confirmed, that she killed herself. She was found alone in her flat with a letter. Her close friends were distraught, but I remember thinking: *How much more could she have gotten from life?* The beautiful books, the beautiful words, the many men, the love affairs, the disappointments, the pain, the war and all the things she saw.

When I met Emerson in Princeton—she killed herself, alone in her apartment in Manhattan—she reminded me of a more raw Gellhorn. She did not have Gellhorn's beauty, but she was clever and smart and lived by herself in a lovely house, surrounded by male friends and admirers. I loved the fact that a male reporter I knew who had reported with her in Vietnam called her a "pain in the ass." I loved any woman who irritated the male press corps, who was strong enough to be described like that.

I loved these women, and what they stood for. They lived alone and played alone and worked alone in a world that did not like women to do that. I wanted to learn from them how to do it. I wanted to be like them, and not—as much as I loved and admired my mother—like the women in my family.

But the thing about these amazing women was that they did not hand out their secrets, or directions for how to live one's life because, I suppose, they did not know. I learned no secrets of how to live my own life without a map from either Emerson or Gellhorn (or even Gloria Steinem, whom I met one winter morning in Manhattan, beautiful in silk pyjamas and bare feet, a few days after her sixtieth birthday), except something I had once read that Gellhorn had written: "I always leaped before I looked."

And this was how I was having my baby. There was no birth plan, no name choice, no knowledge of how to change a diaper, breastfeed, prepare a bottle or even live with the father of my baby. Gellhorn would have coped, I thought. And I could cope.

My shell-shocked husband arrived back in London from Africa the day before Christmas Eve. I was now more than six months pregnant, and he was joining me before we moved together to Paris.

He was gutted, exhausted. And while he seemed joyful and exuberant at seeing me and touching my stomach, he seemed grief-stricken about leaving Africa. He was cutting short his three-year contract. He had closed up the lovely mango-strewn house in Cocody, the place he had loved and decorated with so much pride with teak tables, ivory inlaid mirrors and bright fabrics, and packed his things. He was happy to be home—but he looked so incredibly tired.

Looking back, I wish I had seen how thin he had become,

how much he was trying to hide all the turmoil that he had left behind. I did not see it. I only saw someone who was in love, who took care of all the details. But do we ever see things that we really don't want to see?

He stopped in Paris first, dropped his bags and went to Hermès to buy me leather gloves lined in cashmere for Christmas. He called me from the Gare du Nord. "In three hours, I am going to see my baby!"

On Christmas Eve, we went to midnight mass. We ate caviar with a friend and went to bed, and on Christmas Day went to two separate turkey dinners. I began to pack, quietly folding the gifts friends had given me from the shower, unable to imagine a baby fitting into the blue-striped summer outfits, or the white Petit Bateau snowsuit.

After New Year's Eve we bought our train tickets to France. By now, my own flat was empty except for the bed, and we closed the door and locked it, turning the heat low. We took an afternoon train, and arrived late, in the freezing rain. I remember thinking that this was the beginning of a new life, but no matter how much I tried I could not, in any way, imagine what it was going to be like.

Bruno fell asleep on the train and when he woke up he told me that he'd dreamed he saw the baby's face.

There was sleet on the ground, grey and molded into the pavement. That night, with our bags and the key to the new flat, we took a cab to rue du 29 Juillet. But the elevator was not working. I sat on the bottom of the stairs, and looked up at the six floors above me with terrible hesitation.

"Let's go," Bruno said, hauling the suitcases on his shoulder like a mule, and pulling me up after him. At every floor, I stopped to pant. Even breathing had become impossible.

O. was in Italy, but he had sent a friend—a cool, blonde Frenchwoman with an elegant ponytail—to oversee our arrival. She was thin and brisk and abrupt, and, in retrospect, no doubt stunned by the sight of an immense pregnant woman at her door. Her face was heavily angled, planed, without softness or warmth. She eyed me suspiciously and spoke only to Bruno, explaining how to work the heating and the washing machine. She was as chilly as the ice outside on the balcony.

I walked through the rooms which were still full of O.'s things; nothing had been moved to make way for our arrival. A bright yellow sofa remained, as did the three sofas in the dining room. I sat on the bed, still made up with someone else's sheets, and suddenly it washed over me how irresponsible it was to move to a foreign country where I knew no one two months before my baby was due.

And the elevator did not work, and I was out of breath and the cough I had had for the past month was making me bend over double. When I came back into the room to listen to the woman's instructions, she broke off, mid-breath, and stared at me as if I had cholera. The flat that had enchanted me in August suddenly looked dirty and utterly uncharming.

I sat on yet another sofa in a corridor and tears rolled down my cheeks silently. The room was blurry. I did not have a tissue. The woman looked at me, more in annoyance than in alarm. Bruno said helplessly, "She's pregnant," and the woman replied something, and from that moment on, they both ignored me. I took my backpack and began to unload it, doubting there was space for my books, let alone the forty boxes on their way from Africa and England.

"Why isn't the furniture moved?" I asked her, for the first time addressing her directly. She stopped and stared at me. We were like two cats confronting each other, and I thought, *Oh no, this is how it's going to be with all French women.* Everyone I knew had warned me about them, about the competition, about the lack of sisterhood. But Ariane was my best friend, and there was no one more French than she was.

"If you want an unfurnished apartment," she said finally, "then go rent an unfurnished apartment."

"It's dirty, it was meant to be cleaned," I said. "And there's so much junk and we're never going to be able to move in, and the baby is coming in a month . . ."

"It will be fine," Bruno said, shifting a chair. He too looked shocked at the state of it, but he was more diplomatic than me.

"But I told him to put his stuff away, and why, at least, could he not have thrown away the piles of newspapers . . ."

"It's fine. Really. It's fine." He began to smoke.

The woman finally left, kissing him on both cheeks jovially and glaring at me.

"Don't worry about it," he said. "But you were a little hostile."

He took my hand and brought me out on the balcony. It was cold and rainy, and the plants and the grapevines on the terrace that were alive in August when I saw the place were now dead. Beneath us, Paris looked terribly cold and lonely.

I counted on my fingers the three people I really knew in this entire city. In Notting Hill, I knew a hundred. Why didn't we have the baby in London, then move to Paris? Why hadn't I thought this through? Why hadn't I taken the advice of a Norwegian colleague, a beautiful and rather pragmatic reporter who once told me she would never marry someone who was not her nationality. An affair, yes, but not marriage. Never marry outside your culture. It's just too complicated.

But Bruno and I had thrived on complications.

On the terrace, he pointed to the clock at the Musée d'Orsay, and said it once was a train station, and told me that he had climbed onto the roof with his friends when it was being rebuilt. We could see all the way down to the Place de la Concorde. He pointed to the outlines of the Louvre still visible, the carefully sculpted labyrinth where, in a few years, our little boy would play.

"You see? It's beautiful. It's a beautiful city. And we are going to have a beautiful life. You'll see."

I believed him. Because I was in Paris, because I was in love with someone I had met in a war zone, and had never really lived with before under normal circumstances, or under any circumstances, for that matter. But most of all I believed him because I was about to have a baby and what choice did I have? He handed me a tissue to dry my eyes. I nodded to him, and took his hand. It was leaping before looking.

CHAPTER 6

Birth

The public hospital where I was to give birth was chosen because it had the best neonatal unit in France and mine was deemed a high-risk pregnancy.

Like the apartment, it was dirty. And crowded. And it was unfriendly. Sour coffee came from a machine in the lobby and you had to bring your own pillows and tea kettle. But the doctor who would deliver our son was famous for his skill, and had a Zen-like office with Buddha heads and statues of African fertility gods, and was writing a book about the bond between fathers and sons. If anything went wrong—which was what Bruno was gloomily expecting, because in our world, things always went wrong—I would be safe.

Professor F. had more or less retired from active work, and

spent most of his time writing books and lecturing around the world, but he occasionally delivered a baby. To convince him to take our case, we had gone to see him early on in the pregnancy, right after I had gotten back from five months in Iraq, and Bruno was on a break from Africa.

We waited a long time in his antechamber, and I read old copies of *Paris Match* while Bruno went outside to smoke. When F. called us in, I saw the kindness in his face. He asked about our lives, and Bruno began to talk and talk, nervously, about our work in conflict zones, about the time I disappeared in Kosovo and how he thought I was dead; the time Grozny fell and he thought he would never see me alive; and how he had been beaten up by crowds in Africa. About how we met, how we lost each other, how we found each other, how we strived to have this baby.

"It's a beautiful story," the doctor said, and it must have convinced him we were sufficiently difficult because he took on my case.

He put me on the table and did an ultrasound. He warmed his hands and rubbed jelly on me and moved the wand over my stomach. There was a heartbeat, a small one because the baby was only ten weeks old, the size of an apple seed. But it was alive.

I had lain on these tables and seen, too many times, the look on the doctor's face when he moved the wand and realized the baby was gone. "Tell me what it is," I had once begged an Indian technician in an emergency room in New Jersey when the baby I was carrying was thirteen weeks old. I saw the blank look on her face.

"I'll just go and get the doctor."

"Is my baby all right?"

"I'll just go and get the doctor."

But now, there was a heartbeat. We stared at the screen and there was a tiny pumping heart. And suddenly, Bruno was crying.

The doctor did not seem surprised, but I was. My husband had climbed the Eiffel Tower with ropes and outstayed everyone in the Côte d'Ivoire when the fighting was at its worst. There was that hike through the mountains with the love letter in Kurdistan. I had never, ever seen him frightened.

"What is it?" I said. "He's alive, see?" I pointed to the screen.

Then he said, "The baby is so big," and wiped his face. In fact, the baby was tiny. But I knew what he meant, and so did the professor, who said nothing, just swabbed the ultrasound wand clean of the gel and told me not to eat too much sugar and to be careful.

"This is real," I said as we climbed into the taxi to drive back to Paris. "This is really happening."

It was so big.

And so began our new life in Paris.

Usually the expats in Paris gave birth at the American Hospital in Neuilly, or at chic private clinics in the 16th with french doors that opened onto gardens. One of my American friends had been born in the American Hospital herself, forty years earlier, and delivered all three of her boys there. She told me, laughing, of the menus presented to you when you were about to go into labour, with the choice of wines, and the croissants freshly baked on the premises.

You had a private room. You could give birth screaming in English if you chose to, and people would understand you. Bruno and I went head to head: I wanted to give birth at the American Hospital because it felt safe, and I was feeling terribly unsafe. I missed my mother and my girlfriends; I missed the chemist in London who had known me for a decade, and mixed special cough syrup just for me, and the newsagent, and the grocery store on Elgin Crescent. I missed being someplace where people knew who I was.

"There is no way that our baby will be born here," he said after checking out the surgical unit, which was minimal compared to the French state hospitals. "If something goes wrong, they are going to move you to a hospital you really don't want to be in—like Hotel Dieu." Hotel Dieu was the Victor Hugo-esque hospital where the prisoners from local jails were brought in in chains, and where crowds of people waited in draughty rooms for hours to see a doctor.

Combined with my blood-clotting disorder, which the doctors feared would cause me to haemorrhage during the birth, there was the metal stitch I had had inserted after Israel, to keep the baby firmly locked inside. There was also the problem of my age, which seemed young in New York, but ancient in France where women began their families in their twenties, and where, at thirty-five, you were considered old. And so it was decided, early on, that we would use the Zen doctor and his hospital.

A few weeks after we arrived in Paris, shortly after the Polish painters rolled up their dust sheets and closed the cans of white paint, after we stored O.'s things in a barn outside of Paris, after we painted everything so it was white and clean, after we finally bought a piece of furniture from IKEA on which to change the baby (but I forgot to buy diapers), the SAMU—the French paramedics—arrived for the first time at rue du 29 Juillet.

It started in the early evening. I stood in the bathroom, holding my toothbrush, and began to cough. And cough. And cough, so that I could not stop and could not breathe. I leaned over the sink, and suddenly I heard something pop inside me, and felt a sharp bone sticking in my chest. Later I found out that one of my ribs had become distanced from the muscle from the strength of my cough, and the pain was excruciating.

Bruno found me on the floor, my arms wrapped around my middle. He pulled me to my feet, but I could not straighten my body—the bone was sticking into my skin. "Lie down," he said, but I could not. I stood as best I could while he called 15—the number for the SAMU, the paramedics, and then, hanging up the phone, rubbed my back.

The SAMU arrived within minutes, a man from the Antilles and another thinner, greyer one, and they led me, hunched, into the elevator, which was thankfully now working. But the three of us could not fit in the tiny space—I was that large—so the Antillean man came with me, clearly terrified, and the other one took the stairs with Bruno.

"Ça va, Madame, ça va," he said, trying to comfort me. "Respirez! Soufflez!" But breathing hurt too much.

They strapped me in the ambulance bed, and Bruno shouted that he would take his moto.

"Don't leave me," I said, and he touched my face.

"Five minutes and you are at the hospital."

On my back, I watched the lights of Paris above me as we drove down past Pyramides, then on to rue de Rivoli, past the Louvre, across the bridge, and on to one of the islands in the Seine.

Inside Hotel Dieu were drunks, shouting crazies, a man holding an arm with a deep gash, dripping blood. They all stared at me, this distorted figure twisted in half, like one of Victor Hugo's characters. For once, I was happy to be in France, happy that the doctors were so good, that the nurses here who X-rayed me tried to soothe me, and told me they knew how much it hurt.

My doctor told me that I had torn a muscle that connected the ribs, and one of the ribs was out of place, dislocated, floating around somewhere in my body. She apologized: even if I were not pregnant, there was little they could do about broken ribs, but as I was pregnant, all she could do was wrap me to try to stabilize the bone.

Tiny and birdlike, she worked quickly, binding my upper body in elastic bandage, wrapping me round and round like a mummy, and telling Bruno to buy a warming pad from the pharmacy. But she could not give me any painkillers because of the blood clotting and because she said they would go into my bloodstream and affect the baby.

"I'm sorry," she said, and genuinely seemed to mean it. She pressed her hand against mine. It was tiny, like a doll's hand. "*Courage.* Your baby is coming soon."

The SAMU had left, so we got a taxi home. It was nearly dawn. Since the time I had held my toothbrush while preparing to get into bed, an entire night had passed.

The faint colour was coming back to Paris' streets, even on this cold winter morning, and there were people moving quietly, going to work, the early shift. There was something oddly comforting about that, life going on. I kept my hand on the place where my rib should have been, and watched as we passed the Ile Saint-Louis, Châtelet, down rue de Rivoli and past the Café Welcome with its orange-and-red walls, and back to our apartment. I went to bed and stayed there.

A week passed, and the coughing did not stop. I could not sleep and grew heavier and less agile. I had one pair of boots I could slip on and off, but that was about it. When I coughed, the rib shifted—I could feel it moving under my tight skin—and I would breathe sharply, the pain worse than anything I had ever felt.

One day, it was so uncomfortable that I sat willing the baby to come out, so that my body would return to normal, wishing that I could take a painkiller or a sleeping pill, and fall into darkness, obscurity, where there was no pain, only sleep.

"I know you want him to come," Bruno said, "but he's not ready yet." He tried to lift my spirits with lemon tarts and lemon tea, the only thing I could stomach. He took me for walks around the Place du Marché Saint-Honoré and let me lean on his shoulder. He guided me by the elbow and remained constantly optimistic. The more difficult I became, the more patient he seemed to be. I was aware of how badly I was behaving, like a spoilt and miserable teenager. But it was the first time since I was a child that I depended on someone else, that I was out of control. I did not like it.

One day, Bruno arrived home with news: I had to meet the *sage-femme*—the midwife—who would assist the birth. She was supposed to be magical, recommended by the Zen doctor, and she saw women at a famous hotel in Versailles where she guided them in the water, like bloated balloons, through various prenatal exercises. It was meant to be a surprise, Bruno's treat for me; a trip out of the apartment where I was confined, a swimming pool and the cameraderie of other pregnant women.

We borrowed a car from a friend and set out, freezing because the heater did not work. The *sage-femme* introduced me to the other women, all of them slender with tiny bumps that protruded from their black nylon swimming costumes. The *sage-femme* asked me pointedly: "How much sugar are you eating each day?"

"Sugar? I don't eat sugar." I imagined someone eating spoonfuls of sugar from a sack, or Bruno eating Nutella from a jar with a spoon.

"Because in France, we don't gain more than twenty pounds."

I told her about my enforced bed rest, how I had exercised my whole life and was forbidden to do so during my pregnancy. "To be honest," I told her, "I don't care what I look like now, I just want a healthy baby. I don't want to starve myself, or go on a diet during my pregnancy. I can do that after." After, I added, I stopped breastfeeding.

"You plan on breastfeeding?" I told her I was. She looked at me. "Because, in France, most women don't. It ruins your breasts."

I came from a culture where it was practically criminal not to breastfeed, but I was already having misgivings.

"OK," she said, regarding me as some strange Anglo-Saxon species, "get in the pool."

I climbed into the freezing water with the other women, who seemed pleasant enough and who looked at me sympathetically. One of them spoke English. "I worked in New York," she said conspiratorially, as if to say: *I know how shocking our culture is to you.*

The midwife stood at the edge of the pool like a drill sergeant. "OK, now race! See who can get to the other side first!"

Even when I was not pregnant, I did not like the idea of racing. I thought one of the things about pregnancy was the escape from the competitive life I had lived before—racing against deadlines, trying to get the story before my counterparts on other papers.

"I'm not racing," I said. "I'll swim, but really, I don't want to race."

She shrugged, and the other women paddled viciously. I did some slow laps, but as my skin was turning blue, I climbed out of the pool.

The midwife turned to look at me. "Where are you going?"

"Home," I told her, wrapping a towel around the huge bump that was my baby.

She looked at me coldly. "Are you ready for your birth? Do you know about the options for pain relief during labour? We're discussing that next."

I shrugged. I assumed I would have a natural childbirth, that I was not going to bring my child into the world drugged. "I guess I'm ready." I left her and the poor paddling women, as ready as I would ever be.

At thirty-two weeks, I could not stop coughing. I sat at my dressing table applying eyeliner and blusher because, even while pregnant, French women looked pretty. I spent time lying on the sofa with a blanket over me, and Bruno would light the fire while I read. I waited for my final check-up with Professor F.

We took a taxi to Hôpital Antoine-Béclère, passing Porte d'Orléans, the cinemas, the brasseries, and then the grey suburbs: kebab stalls, betting shops, Arab fruit and vegetable markets. Wet snow and low-hanging grey skies.

Why, at the happiest moments of my life, was I filled with such immense melancholy, such a profound sense of sadness? I was married to someone who loved me fiercely. I was having a baby, at last, who would be much loved, and was much desired. Yet my thoughts were blackened, ashes, coal. My sister said, "It's in the genes. We come from a long line of melancholics. Remember Daddy?" And I suddenly remembered my father on summer afternoons in our beach house, lying down for a siesta but not sleeping, his eyes open, listening to the distant sound of foghorns.

"What are you thinking of, Daddy?" I would ask, coming into his room.

"Leave your father alone, he's resting," my mother would say. "Go out and play."

And it was February and my sister added, rather cheerfully: "February is suicide month. Everyone kills themselves in February." She went on to list our aunts, our cousins and various family members who had died in February. "And Sylvia Plath stuck her head inside an oven," she added. "Because of the cold."

The taxi dropped us outside the hospital, and Bruno bought a coffee in a small plastic cup from a machine. As we rode up the elevator, he turned to me and there was such happiness on his face. He said, "The next time I go up in this lift, it will be to see my baby."

But inside the maternity wing, the Zen doctor was not at all happy. He sat frowning behind his huge desk, fingering his pen. The African sculptures suddenly looked menacing.

"You are very, very fragile," he said. "Not in good shape to give birth." Frankly, he added, he did not know how I was going to push to get a baby out with my ribs broken. And he was perplexed. The cough, he reckoned, was some rare thing I had picked up on my travels: an amoeba, a bug, something infiltrating my system like al-Qaeda infiltrates weakened villages in Pakistan. Perhaps from the dirt in Iraq? He stared at my chart while the muscles in Bruno's face tensed. They spoke in rapid French.

"I'm sorry," the Zen doctor said at last, "but I want you to stay here."

"For how long? I want to go home."

"Until the baby comes. I'm sorry, I know it's not pleasant," he said. "But it's for the best. I have to watch you."

He filled out papers and ordered a battery of tests. He sent me down one floor to the pulmonologist who tapped my chest and back and looked confused. "Possibly TB? When was your last visit to Africa?" he asked, and sent me to the bowels of the hospital for chest X-rays.

The X-rays came back clear on tuberculosis and cancer, and then I was sent for more blood work: for HIV, malaria and other infectious diseases. "Sorry, I know this hurts," the nurse said, seeking out my collapsed veins to slide a large needle under my skin. "What terrible veins!"

"It runs in my family," I said miserably. Like the melancholy and the depression, that too—deep veins that resisted every blood test, making taking a vial of blood agony—was a gift from my family, inherited. My mother and I had simple blood tests and emerged with bruises the size of oranges.

The tests went on all day. Whooping cough, polio, cholera, cancer of every part of my body. I was tested for diseases that I thought had disappeared in Victorian times. An immunologist came to interview me, to try to find the bug hiding somewhere in my system. I climbed onto and off five or six examining tables that day, and everyone poked my ribs and touched my stomach and took my blood pressure and made me cough so that my breath was short.

"Cough!"

"Cough again!"

"Move on your side. On your back! On your side!"

"Give me your arm for a little blood test. This one won't hurt, promise. A little scratch." Everything in French. Medical French. Clinical French. I yearned for someone to speak English to me.

After all the tests came back, and all the doctors conversed and decided they did not know what it was, they put me in the isolation ward. It was at the end of a long, dark corridor and there was no one else there; I felt terribly lonely.

Bruno left for a few hours and came back with a new tea kettle because when I asked the nurse for a cup of tea she stared back at me blankly.

"No."

"What do you mean, no?"

"We bring drinks at mealtimes. You must wait."

Bruno also brought me a pillow, a pale green silk pillowcase I loved, some chocolates and my computer and books.

"I'm not supposed to eat sugar," I said.

"Oh, fuck that, you're pregnant." He went down to the reception and argued with the staff to get the TV turned on. "Anyway, I would love you if you were a hundred kilos."

"I'm not far off."

He made me laugh. He took care of the endless paperwork involved with giving birth to a baby in the French state system. The more complicated it got, the more energized he became.

"Now we are in emergency mode," he said more than once. *My God*, I thought, *he is still addicted to adrenalin.*

Meanwhile, more doctors came in and stuck their hands up my silk nightgown. A team of medical interns came in. A tropical disease specialist too. "It's probably something you picked up in Iraq," said the immunologist. "I'm sure it's from the soil."

"If that's the case," I said, "then why don't all Iraqi women have it?"

He shrugged. "You're foreign. Your system isn't used to it."

Someone else thought it was a rare form of asthma. Someone else wanted to put me on steroids. Professor F., who headed the diagnostic team that surrounded my bed every day with helpful but puzzled faces, kept checking my metal stitch, which I could feel straining every time I breathed. I caught them discussing that it would be impossible for me to give birth in this state.

"I don't want a caesarean," I said one afternoon. "Absolutely not, under no circumstances."

"We don't know till the labour starts how the baby will come out," Professor F. said calmly. "But I will try."

In the end, they could not work out what the cough was. The Greek immunologist who came and monitored all the machines around me thought it might be an allergy, so after a week, they let me go home. That's when I realized medicine was not an exact science. They only do what they can.

"The truth is," the Greek said, "all we can do is relieve your symptoms. I actually have no idea what is wrong with you." I was given packets of various drugs and I did not bother asking what was inside them.

The day I was leaving the isolation wing, I woke early,

before dawn. I heaved myself out of bed, feeling the cold floor under my bare feet. There was no one else on the ward, no other high-risk patients but me, and I thought all the nurses must be sleeping. I could see a blue light coming from a television set in the staffroom, but there was no sound. I stood by the window watching the night seep away and the morning begin. It had started to snow. As I stood in the cold, barefoot, I could see the first people coming to work in the near dark, blowing on their hands to warm them. The snow was so white, so pure and so new. It made me happy.

The ashes inside my head seemed to be fading away. I knew then, for the first time since the pregnancy had begun, for the first time since I started war reporting and entered cities under siege and walked with rebel armies, that everything was going to be all right. The fear that had lain dormant in me like some foreign invasion was gone. The baby was going to live, the cough was going to go away, the rib would heal, and Paris would be fine. I was lucky to be here, lucky to be pregnant, lucky to have Bruno.

I stared at the snow and felt, for the first time, peaceful.

Then I went to my cold room in the isolation ward, and slept.

CHAPTER 7

Greetings

Luca arrived after lunch. The SAMU came to our fifth-floor apartment on 5, rue du 29 Juillet in the middle of the night a few days before the feast of St. Valentine. It was the same unlucky two men, even more nervous this time because my waters had broken. I had gone into labour, but I still had the metal stitch, and the baby's head now pushed against it, trying fiercely to break out. This time I was not crying; I was screaming. I leaned against the french windows overlooking the Musée d'Orsay and howled.

"Madame, please," pleaded the Antillean SAMU, trying to take my arm. "Please don't scream." The two of them led me into the lift, bent over. They got me down the lift, into the ambulance and to the hospital, screaming the whole way. It was near dawn and they drove like Frenchmen: brutally fast, occasionally bumping me up in the air, and I would have fallen off the cot in the back had they not strapped me down with old-fashioned leather straps and a buckle. One drove, and the unfortunate one, the soft-spoken Antillean, had to stay in the back and hold my hand, trying to comfort me, and failing. Earlier, I heard them talking to Bruno: the baby was coming fast, they said, and they would bring me to Hotel Dieu, the closest hospital.

"*Non.* You WILL NOT bring her to Hotel Dieu," he said. "We're going to Béclère."

"But it will take us an hour, and she is in terrible pain."

"Béclère," Bruno said with insistence. "She needs her doctor."

He drove alongside the ambulance on his motorcycle at 120 kilometres per hour, sticking close so that I could see his eyes beneath his helmet.

I had a tiny suitcase and we had remembered to bring our iPod. Think about Bach, I told myself as we drove. Think about the Beatles. Think about conjugating French verbs. But I couldn't forget about the stitch. I screamed and screamed every time the baby's head jutted against the metal holding my cervix closed. When we reached the hospital, the SAMU deposited me with a nurse, and ran away quickly, wishing me luck. I saw the relief when they handed me over to the hospital. I could not blame them.

The hospital at 5 a.m. was empty except for a very young Arab girl with a headscarf and a huge belly. She was alone, leaning on a chair. A nurse came and made me lie down and brought a huge pair of scissors that looked like hedge clippers. She said she was going to cut the stitch.

I drew back. "I want a surgeon," I said.

"There is no surgeon," she replied calmly. "I can do this. I just have to cut the metal. Be still and it won't hurt."

"No!" I screamed. Now I did want the American hospital, and an English-speaking nurse and a doctor who played golf. I wanted it to be clean and easy. I wanted a birth plan, a blue layette and my mother.

"Fine," the nurse said curtly. "Then I won't cut it." She walked out of the room as another contraction came, and the baby pushed harder against the stitch.

"If I were you," Bruno said, from where he was standing somewhere near the door, "I would stop acting like a princess, and I would let her do it." He went to the hallway to get her, and she came back, miffed and slightly smug, and cut the stitch.

She pulled out a metal contraption that looked like a small, bloody bear trap. Gruesome though it looked, it didn't hurt after all.

"Better?" she said, winning her moral victory.

"Better," I gasped. A contraction hit, hard. Suddenly I did not want a natural childbirth. I wanted drugs.

The midwife arrived. It was not the swimming *sage-femme,* but a young woman with dark hair called Nathalie. She had just come back from Australia. She carried a tray and said, slightly embarrassed, that she was going to shave me.

"You can't be serious," I said; this seemed to be my catch-phrase for every aspect of giving birth in France.

"I know it is not something you do in England or America," she said in careful English. "But we prefer it." She had a can of shaving cream and one of those pink plastic razors that come in six-packs.

"Then go ahead." I had given in to the fact that giving birth did not involve keeping my dignity.

"Don't look, please," I said to Bruno. My mother had warned me the week before not to let my husband watch the birth. "Better that they come in after you brush your hair and are sitting up in bed with a pretty bed jacket and lipstick," she said, as if I were in a movie from the 1950s.

More contractions. "Fuck!" I screamed.

Bruno, a bit embarrassed by my outburst, left the room to smoke.

Nathalie snapped on rubber gloves. An Italian anaesthesiologist, pretty in a low-cut blouse under her white coat, asked me if I wanted an epidural while there was still time, then made me lie on my side and put the needle in the base of my spine.

"Give me a lot," I said. I had forgotten that I wanted a natural birth.

"You don't want to feel enough to push?"

"I don't want to feel any pain." My mother, aside from sitting up in bed with her pink quilted bed jacket and her cigarette, had been knocked out cold during all of her births. "It's what they did in those days," she said. At the time I thought it barbaric. Now, struggling against the waves of pain that were so deep it felt as though I had broken bones, I wanted relief.

Aside from his cigarette breaks, Bruno stayed with me the whole time. As soon as the epidural kicked in, I grew dreamy.

We laughed and laughed. We listened to jazz. We fell asleep, me on my narrow bed with tubes running in and out of my back and monitors everywhere, and Bruno with his head on the table and his exhausted eyes.

The midwife came in and out, checking the dilation, but Professor F. did not appear until lunchtime, when the baby decided to come out. Again, he looked worried, and took Bruno aside. "What is it?" I said, trying to sit up and failing.

"Nothing." Bruno came back and stroked my hair. "You're going to push soon."

Then it was past noon. I could tell by the way the light was falling on the table where I was lying, and I desperately wanted a glass of water.

"It's time," Professor F. said gently to me. "He's going to come out soon." They shifted the stirrups higher. I felt like a frog. *I should have done more yoga,* I remember thinking.

Then came a blur of nothingness. I felt no pain below my waist, only a pressure. The midwife, Bruno and the professor were somewhere near my feet. They were shouting at me in French to push. They shouted louder; I was not pushing correctly. "Not with the eyes! Not with the eyes!"

But something was wrong. Bruno came and took my hand. "Please, darling, try harder. The baby's stuck. He needs to get out. Try to push with your breath."

I pushed, but the baby did not budge. Professor F. muttered something to Bruno, who nodded, and he went to another room and came back with what looked like a portable vacuum cleaner. He was saying something about a ventouse. The music changed from Charlie Parker; now it was Julie London singing "My Heart Belongs to Daddy." Bruno made a startled noise: "I see his head." Then a minute later, he said in a strange and delighted voice, "He has your hands!" The doctor reached inside with the vacuum cleaner and scooped the baby out. Our longed-for baby was born.

My little boy was terribly still. I don't remember him crying, but he must have when the doctor whacked him. He was covered in white fluid, and his eyes were closed. He was very small. Apprehensively, I reached out my arms, because that's what you are supposed to do, but I felt frightened of the white stuff all over him.

"Is he dead?" I said.

"No, of course he's not dead," said Professor F.

Later, I wondered why this was the first thing I thought of. I remember thinking I was supposed to cry, that is what new mothers did, so I closed my eyes and two obligatory drops slid down my cheek. Professor F. seemed to approve and handed the naked bundle to me.

"Hold your son," he said. Then to Bruno, he motioned towards the iPod and Julie London warbling: but my heart belongs to . . . Daddy! "He's going to be a blues man," the doctor said, grinning.

They moved him on top of me, near my deflated stomach. I was shaking, from cold, from the epidural, and because I was afraid I would drop him. Was this my baby? It had not quite registered. Wasn't I supposed to feel a sweeping recognition that this was my flesh and blood? That this was my offspring? Wasn't I supposed to feel a rush of undying, undiluted love?

I did not. I felt someone tugging me, trying to get the afterbirth out, and I felt confused. Suddenly, the room was full of people. Someone took him from me, and I did not resist. Two nurses led Bruno away with the baby to wash him. Someone else was noting the exact time of birth. Someone else was down by my legs shouting something about the placenta. There were a few other doctors, a few strangers wandering around as though nothing had happened. For me, everything had happened.

"What is his name?" a North African nurse with a clipboard asked. We had not decided the name. Bruno wanted to call him Geronimo or Pinocchio. Pinocchio because Gepetto wanted a little boy more than anything in the world and we both believed, more than anything, in the truth. I wanted to call him Costantino after my grandfather, or Vincenzo, after my father.

"Luca," we both said, once Bruno had come back into the room with the baby. Luca was the only name we had agreed on. Luce, Luca, the bringer of light. We looked at each other and laughed. "He's called Luca." Later Bruno would register him as Luca Costantino Pinocchio Girodon di Giovanni. The nurse wrote it with the French spelling, Lucas.

"No, Luca: L. U. C. A.," Bruno said. "No S."

After a while, they carried Luca in and they handed him to me again. His white rabbit suit was too big because he was seven weeks early and weighed only 1.9 kilos. I wrapped both arms around him. "I'm afraid," I whispered to the small lump that fit into my hands. "You've got to help me out, because I am really, really afraid."

Bruno had always told me, "Nothing bad can happen when I'm here." I believed him, in that same way you believe your father when he carries you on his shoulders into the waves; the surf is below you, angry and able to swallow you up, but someone else is above it, carrying you. But holding Luca, I felt suddenly frightened of all the things that could happen to this child, all the things I had seen happen to children: disease, war, death.

They wheeled us up to my bedroom, me clutching the baby to my chest, flat on my back, frightened that he would roll off and onto the floor.

"You don't have to clutch him so tight," the nurse said. "He won't go away." But I held him tighter, in his small white rabbit suit. Bruno stood behind us, pushing the gurney, and we went up in the elevator to the third floor.

"He's our redemption," I said, though I was not sure why.

Inside the room, we were three together. My tiny, flawed and perfect family.

CHAPTER 8

Hospital

The baby and I had been in the hospital for more than a week. He was premature, he had jaundice, and he had to lie in a light box, naked except for an eyeshade, the kind they give you on long-distance flights so you can sleep. It physically hurt me to see him flailing and flinching inside the box, blinded and utterly helpless. I still felt as though he were attached to me. "He's cold. Why does he have to be naked?" I wailed to the nurse. "Does he feel the cold?"

"Yes, of course he feels the cold," she said, wheeling him away. The paediatrician was frosty and spoke no English. She addressed Bruno, ignored me, and ignored the tears of frustration that rolled down my cheeks with frequency. I could hear the words *prématuré, jaunisse, faible*. They discussed what extra nutrients he needed, how he should be fed. What

Bruno relayed back to me patiently seemed to be only half of what she was saying.

"Tell me what's wrong," I said.

"Nothing. He's just small. He's just weak."

I lay in bed on my stiff sheets and submitted to all the doctors' check-ups and questions, and I tried to understand the emotional cloud that was suffocating me. I felt, I realized, the same way I had when I was at school and the teacher was doing something I did not understand. I would sit in the back and silently suffer. Eventually, I would become overwhelmed with feeling isolated, cut off, feeling that I did not exist as the teacher scribbled numbers or equations on the blackboard. In strict Catholic convent schools you got sent to the headmistress for this, and I spent a lot of time sitting on the hard bench outside her office.

This is how I felt in the hospital. I existed as flesh and bones, as the woman who had pushed out the baby, but on another level, I existed not at all. No one knew me from my former life. No one knew my father, my mother, or knew what I looked like as a child. The doctor who delivered all of my mother's seven babies was her uncle; we called him Uncle Doc and he treated us for broken bones and inflamed tonsils. I had chosen to leave my home and my family and go as far away as possible, but I had no idea how desperately I would miss them—even the ones long dead and long gone—when I felt the most vulnerable.

One day, an occupational therapist came in to check the baby's lungs. She had round, gold glasses and spoke to me in French, then shifted to English. Her mother was Australian, she said, and she was bilingual. Though I had no connection to this woman, and in my other life we probably would never have met, I felt like she was my only link to my old life.

She calmly explained what was happening to the baby: "He's very early and he has *glare*—liquid—in his lungs." Then seeing my alarm, she added: "He's going to be fine."

Everything seemed mysterious and unavailable to me: the lists of instructions, the medicines, the jabs Luca was getting in his tiny hand that made me flinch—even the first bath that the fat nurse with dyed hair gave him, plunking him down into a basin like a chicken. Bruno stood by her side, lifting out the slippery baby with no apprehension at all. "Hold him, darling, hold him."

"No, I'll drop him. I can't do it."

"Yes, you can," he told me soothingly. "You can do it." Gingerly, he handed me our son. "See? He's so good. He hardly cries at all."

The paediatrician, sensing something was wrong with me, sent in another nurse. This one was blonde and young and she tried to talk to me about *les bébé blues*. "It's normal to cry all the time," she said gently. Then she asked if I wanted or needed antidepressants, and gave me a prescription for birth control, which seemed utterly strange to me, given that I was still raw from childbirth.

The light box sessions, which also seemed strange to me, increased because the *jaunisse* was not going away. In the same way that he had banished me from the Côte d'Ivoire to protect me, Bruno sent me away finally, as he could not stand my pacing and hand-wringing.

He sat alone with the baby for hours, holding his tiny finger through a hole in the glass. He filmed it once, too, with a camera and a night lens and when I look at this eerie greenish film now, I am amazed at the ease Bruno had with a sick baby. He speaks to him gently in French, he laughs with him, he tells him this is what it will be like when he is older and lies on the beach. Bruno seemed, unlike me, utterly comfortable with parenthood. I felt guiltily relieved that at least one of us could cope with it.

"But you are so competent," my friends in London, anxiously calling me to check in, said. "Why is this disturbing you so much?"

"Because it's not me," I said. "It's not my life any more. What if I drop him? Accidentally drop him out of the window?"

"You won't," said one of my friends, the mother of two. She added, laughing: "You sound like a madwoman. Why would you drop him out of a window?"

"I don't know, I just keep thinking that."

I lay in bed and watched the news of Haiti collapsing and I felt something like a failed state myself. Nothing I believed about motherhood was what it really felt like. I was frightened to hold the baby close. The doctors told me not to breastfeed because he was too premature, but I was not happy with the decision. The fat nurse came in and half-heartedly tried to squeeze my breast into the baby's mouth for about five minutes before saying, "It doesn't work. Stick to the bottle."

In a sense, this was not the end of the world. A few days

before I left for the first round in the hospital—the isolation ward—I met a friend, a literary agent, who was also having a baby, her second. She had gained seven kilos—the baby plus an additional three. She was not drinking hot chocolate as I was, but mineral water. She was still working, and she was wearing high heels. She was beautiful, utterly composed and calm. "Are you breastfeeding?" I asked her.

"No way," she said. "It takes all your time, you can't be separated from the baby, and I need to get back to work. And," she added, "you can't sleep." That was the thing that convinced me.

At that point, I had not slept—because of the cough—for two months. I thought of sleep, returning to my normal size, and how much I yearned for it. I left the café, and my half-finished hot chocolate, and walked home to Bruno. He was asleep on the sofa with the lights and the television still on. I had exhausted him with my endless problems, my endless needs.

"I'm not breastfeeding," I said. "I need to sleep, and if I breastfeed, I can't sleep."

He looked surprised and then said, "Whatever. No big deal. It's your choice." My mother-in-law, it turned out, had not breast-fed; neither had the few other French women I knew.

The head nurse reassured me I was doing the right thing: the baby was too delicate.

"It's better for him if you use formula," she said. "And anyway, it ruins your breast tissue." She smiled slyly. "Your husband will be happier."

She then gave me small round yellow pills to dry up the milk. I popped one in my mouth while she was watching, but instinctively spit it out after she left, like a patient interned in a mental hospital. I decided the minute they released me from the hospital, I was going to do it, whether or not they approved.

It wasn't just that response that changed my mind. I began to realise that I was missing out.

My editor phoned from London, and I told her.

"Oh no . . . ," Gill said. "Listen . . . you have to try . . . you'll miss out on the experience."

My friend Sam called. "Did he latch on?" Why was I being asked this by a man, I wondered, and one of my most macho friends, a man I had crouched under fire with in Afghanistan? Why was even he judging me for not breast-feeding? "Because they're like lambs when they're born . . . they do it naturally," he continued.

"Actually," I said, "I'm not breastfeeding. It's not really part of the culture here."

Crushing silence. "Oh."

I hung up the phone and felt worse.

I was missing the experience of motherhood, and I was not sure why. Somehow it was racing past me like a wild horse and I was unable to grab the reins and jump on. Yet everyone else was able to. Passing the other rooms of other mothers, I peeked in and saw them bouncing their tiny babies between their knees. They were feeding them with little bottles of formula with confidence and with no tortured feelings that they were a failure for not breastfeeding. Huge families, small children carrying balloons, grandparents with beaming smiles, husbands opening bottles of champagne surrounded them.

Only an Indian woman who had a room at the end of the hall looked as lost as I did. Her skinny, worried husband had asked the nurses to push a cot into the room so that he could sleep next to his wife. Bruno stayed as long as he could, but I was in Paris, not London. I did not have many visitors.

"Don't leave me alone here," I begged him the first night. "Please don't leave me alone."

"But you're not alone!" he said, pointing to the glass box where the baby slept. "There's this little creature here!"

Two days after I gave birth, on Valentine's Day he brought me champagne and small pastries filled with creamed chicken and smoked salmon, caviar, and blinis, and roses and chocolates. He stayed with me and told me how much he loved me, and held the baby and fell asleep in the chair with him.

At 10 p.m., he got up to leave. I felt, as I always felt when I was left alone with the baby, in a general state of alarm. Bruno took my hand as he was leaving. "You're going to be a great mother. Just do what you feel is right. You won't do anything wrong."

"There's so much I could do wrong . . . the wrong amount of formula, I don't know how to mix it, how to sterilize the bottles, I could drop him in the bath, I might stand too close to the window . . ."

"Not the window again. You'll be fine." He went back to Paris. "I've got to sleep, baby, I've got to sleep. I feel like I'm going to collapse." He had been awake for thirty-six hours, sitting by me while I slept.

After he left, I picked up the baby and I stared at him hard. He had slanted eyes, like his father, and his fingers were long and slender, like mine, but they were still tiny. If I squeezed them, they would break. He had white dots on his nose, that the nurse explained had something to do with coming into contact with the air when he came out of me, into the world. All he did was sleep.

I put him back in the glass box that was his crib, and sat at the edge of the bed, watching him. The crazy thoughts came back into my head. *What if he chokes? How do I feed him? How do I change him?*

The nurse, the fat one who was friendly and had a suburban accent, arrived and took him away. "You need to sleep," she said, looking at my chart. "You're overwrought." She gave me a huge blue pill, which was some kind of sedative, and took the quiet baby to the nursery. This time I did not fight the pill or hide it in the crook of my bed. I gulped it down with water, not caring if it was Thorazine or Prozac or something stronger. I just wanted the anxiety, the fear and the sense of dread to go away.

She wheeled the baby away down the hall in his glass box, the creaky wheels making annoying noises. *They're taking my baby away,* I thought dimly through the drug haze, *and I don't even care.*

I did not sleep right away, but lay on top of the sheets, stoned from the medication. The room was dark except for the blue light of the TV: five French channels and CNN. I

watched the crisis in Haiti growing and saw a crowd of pho-
tographers in Port-au-Prince, and caught the back of the
head of someone I knew well in the crowd: Tyler. I smiled,
thinking of a long trip to Somalia we had taken for a magazine article. The trip when Bruno phoned and said, "Let's get
married. Let's have a baby."

That was my old life. I dimly wondered how quickly I
could get to the Caribbean, to Haiti, if I had to. In the old
days, I would have gotten my passport from my bottom
drawer, taken my summer clothes, then gone to the airport
and bought a ticket. A flight to Miami from Paris was nine
hours, then . . . Wait! I was a mother! I was not going anywhere for a while.

And I was still so weak, and not used to being weak. I
could barely walk from the after-effects of the epidural. I was
sure the pretty Italian anaesthiologist had overdosed me, and
I was grateful for her mistake. I had not felt a thing. My
friend in London was horrified: "You mean you did not want
to feel the pushing?"

"No. Why should I?" I'd had broken bones before, I told
her. I don't need to know what pain is. And the big blue pill
did not put me to sleep, but it seemed to mellow me, as if my
anxieties were wrapped in cotton wool.

Someone brought dinner, an older woman who spoke
incomprehensible French. She smelled bad and had ugly
mousy brown hair, which seemed glued to her scalp. She
muttered as she arranged the dishes of watery mashed potatoes and a flattened chicken breast and carrots floating in
margarine. She seemed disturbed in some way, her move-

ments violent. She frightened me, like one of the main characters in the big Beatrix Potter book someone had given me
for Luca. A giant rat.

"I can't eat," I told her, and asked for tea. She looked startled, interrupted from her muttering.

"Tea? No tea." She left, still talking to herself. Someone
else came in and said under no circumstances should I get
out of bed because I would fall.

"You're wobbly," they said. "But at least you don't have
stitches. The professor is a genius. You are lucky." Someone
came in with another giant pill, this one green, and a glass of
water. Someone else gave me an injection. I know I should
have asked what they were for, but the truth was I did not
care. The hours floated, the baby cared for by strangers in a
nursery down the hall.

"Now you really must sleep," said the night nurse. And
I did.

Sometime during the night the green pill wore off and I
woke up. I was sore and the place where my drip was connected to my arm ached. I heard a baby crying, several in
fact, in unison, but I instinctively knew that it was not my
baby. I got out of bed, sliding the IV drip still attached to my
arm along with me down the hall as though I was leading a
dog on a lead. I found the nursery and looked for my baby.
But they all looked alike, these strange creatures: small, wrinkled, dressed in too-large jumpsuits, topped off with either
blue or pink knitted caps. Some were screaming and some

had masses of black hair. Did my baby have hair? I had only seen him for a few hours. Was he the baby in the second cot? I peered at the name card which said, "*Caresse-moi,* but only with your eyes." No, that baby was called Adam. The next one was a girl called Chloe. Then there was a Gary—a decidedly un-French name—and a Roman.

Then I saw my baby. All the other babies were lying down, but mine was sitting up in a kind of chair, because he had fluid in his lungs. The nurse had called it *glare,* but no one could translate for me. I had called a French friend in London in desperation. *"Glare,"* she said thoughtfully. "I'm not sure there is a word in English. It's a kind of thick thing in your throat . . . let me think . . . yes, phlegm! That's the word: phlegm!"

My baby was sitting up and was not crying. In fact, he was remarkably still, quiet, calm. Later, everyone would tell me how *"sage"* he was. This baby was slightly cross-eyed and seemed to be staring at his fingers; his lips were pursed slightly, as if he was whistling. While the other infants howled and screeched around him, he seemed utterly content and quiet. It was my Luca.

And then, at that second, I fell in love with my baby. He was really, really mine, and he was alive. He had lived. He had survived. We both had. I asked the nurse if I could hold him. She handed him to me. He cuddled near my broken collarbone, the one I had broken twice when I was eighteen, and instinctively found the bone that stuck up, as though he wanted to make it feel better. He nuzzled into my skin as though he wanted to go back inside me. He reminded me of a small chicken, a capon. For weeks after, Bruno and I called him the capon.

I was, I realized as I stroked him, slowly, completely and utterly in love for the first time in my life. Terrified, but in love.

We had a car seat, a gift from the baby's godfather, one of my dearest male friends who was chosen because he was not a war correspondent, and because he was a grown-up, wore a suit to the office and was responsible. We had a car seat, but no car, which was typical of us. I thought it might be useful to carry the baby around in—I had seen other mothers doing it.

On leaving day from the hospital, Bruno and the taxi driver guided me into the back seat with the baby in the crook of my arm. The driver said it was safer that way, as the baby was too small to fit into the seat, and so he motioned for me silently to hold the sleeping baby tight. Luca's mouth was open and resting on the skin of my neck. He breathed lightly. He hardly ever cried, or opened his eyes, and I would often place my finger under his nose to see if I could feel his breath. In the car, I wound the seat belt around and around us, and locked the door.

I was leaving the hospital a different person than when I had arrived two weeks before, and everything around me seemed intensified. The taxi smelled strongly of the driver's lunch, which sat in a waxy bag on the front seat. The metallic grey of the February sky seemed frostier; the softness of the baby's cheek rubbing against my own; and how easily I cried when people were kind to me. The driver was North

African and young, and he took care not to stop short; not to brake or run through red lights. Bruno rode alongside on his motorcycle. At stop signs, he peered into the window of the taxi and waved. Behind the glare of his eyepiece I saw him smile. We passed the suburban pizza parlours run by Tunisians, the small brick cottages, the discount groceries with boxes of carrots and onions piled outside, and finally the roundabout near Porte d'Orléans, around the lions at Denfert-Rochereau, down Boulevard Raspail with schoolchildren coming home for lunch, across the river and alongside the Tuileries, dusted lightly in frost. He drove up rue des Pyramides and across rue Saint-Honoré and left onto rue du 29 Juillet. Then he opened the doors, unloaded my case and helped me out with the baby while Bruno parked his moto. We were home.

PART TWO

Since dark is what brings out your light

Robert Frost,
"Choose Something Like a Star," 1947

CHAPTER 9

The Domestic Life

I would like to say it was easy, but it was not. I had thought, in my chaotic way, that everything would fall into place the way it did when I wandered into a foreign country or a conflict I had never been in before. But this too was a foreign country, the strangest one that I had ever visited.

When I was seventeen, my parents dropped me and my trunks off at my university dormitory and drove away. "Goodbye, darling," my mother said. "Everything will be fine." And it was. From that moment on, I was alone in my life and somehow I always found the right people, the right place, the right job or bed to sleep in or papers to fill out that would help me not be lost in the world. In the past, I never wanted, or needed, anyone to hold my hand. But in the past, I always reckoned it was just me fighting it out against the world.

The pregnancy and the birth had been new assignments. But now there was a tiny, squirming creature who needed his umbilical cord cleaned and who peed in my face when I took off his diaper. And I did not know how to attach his diaper properly, not as well as Bruno did, who cheerfully whistled as he fed him, bathed him and changed him.

I wanted to protect him from everything. So when I held him, I held him very tight, so tight that any other baby would have flinched. But he seemed, in his instinctual and utterly new way, to understand how desperate I was, and he seemed to love me even more for it.

That night, at home, before he tried to sleep, Bruno wrote to his friends to announce the birth. The translation was:

For nothing in the world would I miss the Rugby World Cup of Six Nations 2004 . . . So I decided on Thursday, 12 February at 4:27 a.m. to wake up my parents, who were sleeping deeply, and get them to help me with my intention to proudly sing "La Marseillaise" as quickly as possible!

After crossing Paris at 132 kph (the speedometer went crazy!) and some insults directed at hospital personnel who did not understand my mother's demands for an epidural (those of you who know my mother's character will understand . . .) and then, I was among you in the world, warm and welcoming (Papa doesn't always believe this but we can talk about it later).

OK, let me introduce myself . . . Luca Costantino Pinocchio (the first one who makes fun of me gets a punch in the nose)

Girodon di Giovanni, son of Bruno and Janine, born 12 February 2004 at 2:59 p.m. and not 3 p.m.

Born into a world sweet and tough, honey and vinegar, tender and merciless . . . that's life!

Please don't hesitate to give me any words of advice that I might need. After all, I am only two days old!

Nice to meet you!

Luca

And then one day, a maternity nurse from England—whom Bruno called Mary Poppins—arrived on the train from London, and on day ten after the birth, miraculously, despite the fact that I had not breastfed since he popped out, my milk suddenly appeared.

Mary Poppins was really called Lesley, and she was a maternity nurse that I had arranged—my one bit of organization—before I was whisked into the confusion of the hospital. She had grey-blonde hair and kept cats, and seemed not to eat at all; she was dieting, she told me. She lived in the south of England and had grown-up children. Bruno went to collect her at Gare du Nord, so she would be with us when we arrived home from the hospital, and she loved the motorcycle ride through Paris. She slept with the baby in the same room, in the canopy bed from Kerala, and she brought with her a device to place under him to monitor his breathing.

"Cot death," I muttered ominously to Bruno. "Something else to worry about."

She brought Luca to me every few hours. She taught me

to change his diaper and clean his umbilical cord. She made me cups of tea, she showed us how to mix formula and heat it, and she wrote in her notebook: "Mother teary."

And she got me to breastfeed, effortlessly. It took five minutes of her guiding the baby's head towards my swollen breast and he latched on. It was that easy. Lesley took out a notebook and made two columns: Left Breast/Right Breast. We wrote down how much he drank, how long and from which breast.

Bruno lit fires, made dinner, did the night shift with the baby. He made the home that he called *la nid de oiseau*—the bird's nest. When I cried, he rubbed my back. He told me over and over how everything would be all right. He called my friends in London one by one and told them to come over to Paris as soon as they could. "She needs you," he said.

He sent my mother a plane ticket. When she quibbled about flying alone, he said he would fly to America and collect her. In the end, she arrived alone. During all this time, he did not sleep. He stayed awake with Luca. When we heard the baby stir, he would gently push me down in bed and go to the room where Lesley was. Later, after she left, he would not let me get up in the night. I was coping as best I could during the day, never letting the baby out of my arms. At night, I collapsed.

"Stay and rest," he would whisper, and pad silently away, taking the baby to the kitchen, laying him on a blanket on the floor, and playing jazz on the radio and singing to him while he made his bottle. I think he feared for my sanity. He told me to go outside, which I resisted. When, a few weeks after birth, I did not fit into any of the tiny tiny clothes in French boutiques, he told me that I was beautiful: "May I remind you that you just had a baby?"

He bathed the baby in the big claw-footed tub and was not afraid he would drown. He also bathed him in the kitchen sink. He took three months off work. He knew how to burp the baby perfectly, while I struggled and was frightened of hitting him too hard. He was the champion diaperchanger—he could do it in cafés, on aeroplanes, on his lap.

We went to Normandy and drank martinis in the bar of a grand old hotel, the baby in a basket next to us. We drove to Bordeaux to see Bruno's parents and the baby slept in a suitcase nestled in blankets. We drove together to thalassotherapy in the south-west, and he helped me into salted tubs of water as I held the baby in my arms. And we drove through Basque villages, stopping for *saucisse* and wine. He took me, always, to churches. As I lit endless candles, praying for protection, he hovered near the door. On Easter Sunday, he took me to a famous church built in the 1500s in St. Jean de Luz to hear the male Basque singers, their voices deep, low and haunting. The baby slept through the whole thing.

Mary Poppins had helped me back into the world. Partially, it was all the equipment that terrified me: the fold-up *poussette*—stroller—that never closed when I needed to get into a taxi, and more mysteriously, the kangaroo sling. She helped me understand the mechanics of each, speaking slowly to me as if I were the child, and once I mastered it by myself, we took

Luca outside for the first time, to Monoprix on the Avenue de l'Opera.

"What if he cries?" I said.

"Then you rock him and he stops."

"What if we need to change him, and we're outside?"

"Then we find a place and we change him. Darling," she said, "you aren't the first woman in the world to have a baby."

"And if he's hungry?"

She reached into the diaper bag and pulled out a bottle of formula. "You sit and breastfeed him or you give him a bottle. No one is going to arrest you."

Still, it would be two years before I could get on a moving escalator with a *pousette,* and three before I could board a plane alone with Luca without having to take Valium.

Mary Poppins left one day in March with a note. Although she had never seemed particularly warm with Luca—she called him "baby" rather than use his name—she told me she thought he was one of the best babies she had ever cared for. The note said this:

THINGS TO CONSIDER

FEEDING

1. SITTING IN A MORE UPRIGHT POSITION WHEN FEEDING, AND HAVE EVERYTHING TO HAND BEFORE YOU START, MOBILE PHONE, DRINK, TV CONTROLS.

2. PERSIST WITH A FEED WHEN BABY "APPEARS" TO HAVE FINISHED I.E. WINDING, CHANGING POSITION, UNTIL YOU'RE CERTAIN THAT HE'S DONE.

3. IF YOU THINK BABY IS STILL HUNGRY AFTER BREAST IS

EMPTY, OFFER 2ND BREAST AND/OR FORMULA. IDEALLY, FEED FROM ONE BREAST AT EACH FEED.

4. ALLOW BABY TO BE HUNGRY BEFORE OFFERING FEED. I.E. COMPLETELY AWAKE BY EITHER TALKING TO HIM, PLAYING WITH HIM OR LETTING HIM CRY A LITTLE.

5. DON'T FEEL GUILTY IF AFTER A STRUGGLE TO LATCH HIM ON YOU WANT TO GIVE HIM A BOTTLE. IF YOU'RE IN A STATE HE WILL PICK UP YOUR VIBES AND BECOME UNSETTLED.

6. AS LONG AS YOUR BABY EATS IT DOESN'T MATTER BY WHICH MEANS HE DOES IT.

WINDING

1. ONE BURP MAY NOT BE ENOUGH, CARRY ON FOR A SHORT WHILE, BUT NO LONGER THAN TEN MINS.

2. BURPING MAY MAKE WAY FOR MORE FOOD.

3. HE CAN LIE DOWN EVEN IF HE APPEARS WINDY, HE WILL EITHER RECTIFY THE PROBLEM BY HIMSELF BY SQUIRMING AND GRUNTING, OR LET YOU KNOW BY CRYING. IN WHICH CASE USUALLY PICKING HIM UP OUT OF HIS CRIB WILL CAUSE HIM TO BURP.

GOING OUT

1. BE READY TO GO BEFORE YOUR BABY FEEDS SO THAT YOU CAN LEAVE AS SOON AS HE'S FINISHED. IF YOU WAIT TILL AFTER HE'S EATEN TIME WILL FLY PAST AND BEFORE YOU KNOW IT IT'S TIME TO FEED HIM AGAIN.

AS LUCA GETS BIGGER, HIS TIME AWAKE WILL INCREASE AND YOU MAY FIND THAT HE EATS AND THEN WILL PLAY FOR A LITTLE TIME AND THEN FALL ASLEEP.

HE IS PROBABLY ONE OF THE BEST-BEHAVED BABIES I HAVE WORKED WITH. I AM SURE THAT LIFE WILL BE FULL OF JOY AND SURPRISES.

HAVE FAITH IN YOURSELF AND YOUR JUDGEMENTS. THERE IS NO RIGHT OR WRONG WAY TO BRING UP YOUR BABY, JUST YOUR WAY.

DON'T LISTEN TO ANYONE ELSE, GO WITH WHAT YOU FEEL IS RIGHT. YOUR BABY IS AN INDIVIDUAL AND NOT MEANT TO BE THE SAME AS ANYONE ELSE'S BABY.

YOU AND BRUNO MAKE WONDERFUL PARENTS. ENJOY.

CHAPTER 10

Mother

Mary Poppins left and my mother, whose name is Kathryn but whom we always call Cat Cat, arrived. Her face when she saw me holding the baby was an expression I had never seen before: a mixture of surprise, joy, sadness, longing, shock and exhaustion from her ten-hour journey. My mother was eighty-four years old when Luca was born, a great-grandmother five times over already, and the mother of seven children, six of them living. She was, and is even as I write this, the most extraordinary woman I have ever met, even if she can be difficult. "And you are not difficult?" she would retort.

Her generation of mothers did not talk openly to their children about their anxieties. Nor did they play with us in the way that parents now play with children. We were meant to behave, to act a certain way, and above all, to conform.

As a mother, she did all the right things: baked cookies, did not work, dressed us in the best clothes and picked us up from music and ballet and football and cheerleading practice. But she was distant to me when I was growing up, particularly in my adolescence, as far away as a creature in the Arctic.

But when Luca arrived, we became close, as close as I have ever been to anyone other than Bruno, for the first time in my life.

Although I sometimes felt, in that way that children in large families do, lost inside my strange, large family, I loved my mother fiercely. But her love, it seemed, was forever divided among seven people: me, my five living siblings and my father.

I was Cat Cat's baby, her seventh child, born when she was forty-two, her last. A sister had died from meningitis a decade before I arrived and before me there were four boys and a much older sister, who was seventeen when I was born. It was a complicated arrangement: so many children, such scattered ages.

Much later, I would realize that perhaps I came into her life at a difficult time, an exhausted time, a time when she would need replenishing, and instead, there was another baby to care for. And yet, once when I was a teenager, she told me woefully, "I so wanted a little girl after all those boys. And then you came."

I remember sitting on a church pew on a wintry Sunday

morning next to my mother and burying my face in her chinchilla coat. The aroma was musky and reminded me of the summer storage cupboard; but I wanted to be as close to her as I could get. I wanted to be inside her skin—it was always soft, and smelled of the cream she used, rosewater and glycerin. I took baths with my mother when I was tiny. I saw her breasts and said, "I want those." I wore her high-heeled shoes and sat at her dressing table—she was the kind of woman who had a dressing table with porcelain perfume bottles and elaborate pieces of jewellery. I loved her smell of Guerlain, of Shalimar. I loved her dark auburn hair and her pink frosted lipstick.

I loved her even when I did not notice how annoyed she was to have me constantly trailing behind her when she wanted to be alone, wanted to be with my father, wanted to be unencumbered.

When I was five or six, before I started school, she would take me to a restaurant called the Hamburger Train. It was a sweet little diner with booths shaped like trains for children. She would order me a hamburger and she would have a cup of coffee. She would light a cigarette—an elegant, long, white-filtered cigarette—and leave lipstick marks on the edges. One day, when we went next door to go food shop-ping at the A&P, she sat me in the cart, in the front part for babies and children. We went through the aisles quickly—everything always seemed to be in a rush because there were other children with other lives who needed attending to—and she put boxes of crackers and pasta and washing powder in the wire cart, and when she got to the meat counter, the butcher, a man called John, whom she told me was a widower (I did not know what that word meant, and when she explained it, I got a terrible fear that she would die too, like the man's wife), flirted with her, and she flirted back. But I was too young to know that then.

When she went clothes shopping at JM Townes, a fancy shop in town, there was a tiny child's theatre inside the shop where she left me alone in a big cushioned chair. They played cartoons, Looney Tunes and Bugs Bunny and Popeye the Sailor Man, so that the mothers could shop in peace. The other children laughed and hooted, but I always sat near the door, fearful that my mother would never come back. When she appeared, her arms full of gift-wrapped boxes in beautiful colours, with curling ribbons and bright paper, I would grab her around her stocking legs, and she would always shake me off. "Calm down, darling," she would say. "Time to go home." But I was a neurotic child, afraid of the dark and being left behind.

My parents drank gin martinis on Saturday afternoons. They drank one each, and smoked a cigarette—in my father's case, it was his one and only all week; he was an athlete and he went running each and every morning. It was their treat, their time to relax and forget about bills, children, chicken pox, the mortgage and the school board. They sat outside our big house in the suburbs and drank the martinis out of frosted glasses. *Where am I?* I wonder now. My brothers are off playing somewhere else, no room for a little sister. I am playing somewhere in the vast backyard, the American backyard with a weeping willow tree and woodlands that sweep back towards streams and unimaginable things, dark things, bad things. Maybe I am in the wood eating the poison berries I have been warned not to eat, but which I pick off the branches and weigh in my hand, wondering.

My parents started preaching fear to me early on. I should not walk for long in the woods by myself—I liked to go there to pick the berries and imagine there were fairies under the bridge—because there were bad people who would snatch me. I mustn't stay alone in the house, because there could be fires or earthquakes or disasters. I must be suspicious, cautious, on guard. Terrible things happened in the world, which was a frightening, large place; it was better to stay at home with my family and my cats and the dog.

When I think of my childhood, my mother is in her forties. She has that thick curly auburn hair which she wore in a fashion called the flip. In the 1960s, she wore Gucci print shifts, skirt-and-jacket suits, high heels and a yarn-like thing that held her hair back. When she exercised to a television programme called *Jack Lalanne,* she wore grey stretch trousers with a hook around the foot. My brother Joe and I would sit and watch her and laugh at her silliness. She never, ever went out of the house ungroomed, although she never had her nails done because she hated her hands. I inherited her hands with their long fingers and so did my son.

She smoked Benson & Hedges 100 Lights, and was naturally beautiful: she wore hardly any make-up, except when she went out in the evening, when she would put on eyeliner with a pencil. She had a gold charm bracelet which my father had given her, heavy with tiny objects that had been presented over the years. Sometime in the future, she would sell it when one of my brothers went into rehab and they needed money.

My mother had wanted to be a girl reporter like Lois Lane on *Superman,* but it was not a respectable profession in the late 1930s when she graduated from high school. Her uncle, who was a doctor and had offered to pay her university costs, would not pay for her to study to become a newspaper-woman. She did not really need to work, but for a short while she did at an insurance company that was renowned for only taking girls from good families, and she saved her money for beautiful dresses, and dated my father. They married, and she worked her entire life as a mother and, first and foremost, a wife. She believed in taking care of her husband and her children.

When I think of her in that frosty haze of my childhood, I think of her in that church on a Sunday, and me next to her in the pew. It's that same memory. I am resting my head on her collar. The softness of the fur comforts me, and she is warm, and for a moment, my mother, who belongs to my father and my five other siblings, belongs only to me.

This does not happen often in my childhood; she is more often than not exhausted when I ask her to sit at my tiny table and have a tea party, or read to me. There are too many children and too many problems. There is my father's melancholia, which hangs over the house in a kind of cloud, but which no one ever talks about. There is my dead sister. My mother told me only once of the aftermath: "I could not get on a bus alone for a year." But she did not often talk about it, and could not bring herself to dive into the sorrow she must have felt at losing a child. When I was small, I would say, "But you have *us*. Why did you need another baby?"

"You don't understand. You won't understand until you are a parent."

For ten minutes during Sunday mass, while my brothers are at the front of the church, altar boys, and my father is lost in thought, I have my mother to myself. It feels magical.

She first saw the baby when I came down the hall of rue du 29 Juillet, holding him unsteadily in my arms.

"Oh," she said. "That must be Luca!" She looked eternally happy.

And so, with the birth of my son, I got my mother back. She taught me so many things in those three weeks: how to cook foods I remembered from my childhood; how to fasten the diaper tighter so it did not explode on the bus; and she sat next to me while I breastfed, even though she had not breastfed any of us—"It's not what we did in those days"— and she wrote in her careful handwriting which breast the baby nursed, and the time.

She taught me how to heat the bottles and how to test the temperature on the back of the wrist. She taught me how to lower the baby into the bath, and how to dress him. And she sat on the sofa, rocking and singing to him, something I am fairly sure that she never had time to do with me.

It was the same as having her to myself in church for those ten minutes. And I was, finally, after so many years of being angry at my mother and angry at my family, at peace. I could see that she loved this tiny baby, how special he was to her.

When my mother left Paris, I left the baby with the new nanny, Raquel, and I went with her to the airport by taxi. I had gotten the Air France representative to take her to the gate, even though she insisted she did not need it and felt insulted that I had asked for it. She was not very agile and the walk to the planes at Charles de Gaulle airport takes half an hour. She relented, we checked her in, I got her boarding pass, and then suddenly, a small Algerian man was there, waiting to take her away.

I was not ready to say goodbye to my mother. "Don't cry," she said in a hoarse voice. She was dressed in ballet flats and a tailored suit and a hat—my mother comes from a generation of women who still dress in suits and hats and elegant shoes when they travel, a hangover from the era when only the wealthy travelled on aeroplanes. Don't leave me, I wanted to say. I only just got you back.

Looking at me in alarm she said, "Don't cry." Then the little Algerian took her away and before I could say, "I won't," he had her through customs, and all I could see was the brim of her hat—she always wore hats, this one was a beautiful leopard hat with a white ribbon. She was gone so quickly, and I was alone in Paris once again. Alone in my apartment with a small, helpless baby.

I felt as forlorn and lost as a five-year-old, as lost as when I was a child and someone forgot to pick me up from school, and one by the one the yellow buses left with children going home, and one by one the other mothers came and then the playground was empty. Surely, it could not have been empty—there must have been a teacher, or a grown-up at least, making sure that there were no strange people around. But I think no one thought like that in those days. In my mind, looking back at a childhood memory, I am alone on the playground waiting for my mother or perhaps it was one of my brothers who was meant to get me, but forgot.

I stood there watching the line of people showing their passports and wheeling large bags and adjusting the straps of their backpacks, and then I sat in one of those plastic chairs for a long time, infinitely sad at her departure.

A large African woman standing near me said, *"Ça va?"* and I said, *"Oui, ça va,"* and she handed me a Kleenex, and I wiped my nose. I cried all the way home on the RER. I cried when I could not manage to get the ticket into the machine, cursing even though it was my own fault; I saw people leaping over the turnstiles, and I almost leaped too, but then the metal gate swung open. I stood on the smelly RER as it ran through the grim suburbs of Paris that no tourists ever see, but which is the real Paris of immigrants and the poor, the displaced; places where people lead lives of real desperation and never get to see the Eiffel Tower; where they finally get fed up that they will never get jobs or a chance at life and they riot and burn cars.

I stopped crying by the time I got to Châtelet, and changed to line 1, and got myself home.

I cried for a few weeks after my mother left, and until I got used to being alone, even though Bruno was very much there, and very aware of my fragility. He made me rest. He continued to do the night shifts. And he tended to me as though I was ill, which in fact I was.

A specialist in post-traumatic stress disorder, which I had been tested for extensively in the 1990s by a Canadian psychiatrist writing a book about war reporters, said I did not have it. Aside from one brutal flashback after the murder of two of my colleagues in Sierra Leone by rebel forces, and weeks of seeing people amputated at the wrist or the elbow, I managed, somehow, to escape a syndrome with which so many of my colleagues had been afflicted. At one point, a psychiatrist in Sarajevo told me that nearly the entire population of the besieged city probably suffered from it.

I had never had nightmares in the years of moving from war to war—perhaps some inner survival mode would not allow me to be introspective enough to see it—but they started now: vivid dreams of burning houses, of people without limbs, of children trapped inside shelters. I thought endlessly of the days in Chechnya when I listened to the helicopter gunships and put my hands over my ears, sure I would go mad from the sound of the bombs. Or the time that I rode on the back of a motorcycle in East Timor and smelled the burning of the houses, saw the terror in people's faces.

Every time something terrible happened to me, Bruno was there to save me. In January 2000, I had gone to Chechnya, knowing what I would find: a brutal war, perhaps worse than what I knew in Bosnia. Before I left, I phoned a friend, a seasoned reporter, Miguel—one of the two who was killed in Sierra Leone—and he told me pointedly that the shelling would drive me to the point of madness. He advised me to ask the Chechen rebels to bring me out at least one week before I reached my breaking point. "Because they won't let you go right away, it will take them a while to organize."

But two days after I arrived with a German photographer, Thomas, the city fell. We were caught in a suburb with the retreating Chechens, who were covered in blood from crossing a minefield to get out. I stood in a freezing school building with my feet sticking to blood on the floor as the lone doctor chopped off limbs with minimal anaesthetic, and I saw the men's eyes open on the table, bracing themselves against the saw.

That night, I gathered with the soldiers in a small wooden house and we told jokes, but there was nothing to joke about. The Russians were circling the village with tanks; by daybreak they would enter and probably waste everything in sight, the way they had wasted villages like Shamaski, nearby, when special forces went in high on drugs and killed and killed and killed.

I was there illegally, without a work permit, without a Russian visa, and there were no aid workers, no UN peacekeepers, no Médicins Sans Frontières. There were Thomas and me, and earlier I had met a French reporter dressed as a Chechen woman, but that was it. There was no way for us to leave the village, and the shelling that was raining down on us was heavy. The soldiers were planning on following the railway tracks in the mountains at daybreak, dragging their dead behind them, and they said we could follow them high into the mountains where it was safer. Thomas thought it was a good idea, but I thought it meant death: for sure the Russians would pummel the column of soldiers, and then us.

I walked through the fields with a young soldier to see the commander. The soldier spoke some English, the kind learned from television. "If you could only see Chechnya in the spring," he said. "The flowers are so beautiful!" Night fell and we looked up at the stars, and I remembered Bruno telling me that I was born under a lucky star. "And it's always there and you are never alone."

Back in the house with the other soldiers, we ate pickled cabbage from a jar an old woman had given us, and bread. I sat on a bench with my arms wrapped around myself from the bitter cold and thought, *All right, this is it. This is really the end.* With the last battery of my satellite phone and no electricity, I filed my story: Grozny had fallen to Russian forces. Then I called Bruno. "I can't get out. I'm trapped here."

"Listen," he told me in the calmest voice, "I can't do anything for you from here. No one can, do you understand? But you have to get out of there, somehow. Find a way to leave that village, don't stay with the soldiers any more. And don't be scared. You are going to live. You have angels all around you." Then he hung up, telling me that saving batteries was more important. "I'll see you soon—do you understand? Now get out of there, fast."

I stood with the receiver in my hand, and disconnected my satellite phone. I spent all night in the potato cellar with the old woman while the shells fell, and then in the morning light, I saw the soldiers retreating in a long column, some angry, some throwing their guns in the snow, dragging the dead. There was so much blood in the snow.

An hour later, the man from Ingushetia who had brought us into Chechnya drove into the compound in an old car. "Get in, get in," he shouted. "Now!" He had bribed the Russians to get through. The old woman dressed me like a Chechen, and someone handed me a baby for me to smuggle out.

"Not a word," the driver said. "You're a deaf mute. This is your baby. We're leaving."

On the way out, we wove through the tanks and he handed each crew money. When we got to the road, he broke into breakneck speed and told me, ridiculously, to put my seat belt on. The baby did not cry at all. I turned to look at the village one last time and saw the tanks moving in.

We found refuge in another village that seemed safe, but which got rocketed a day after we arrived, killing schoolchildren I had seen earlier, walking in the snow with little backpacks. From there, I phoned Bruno.

"I knew you would live," he told me. "The best reporter is the one who gets out to tell the story. And also," he added, "there are the angels."

Then, and later, I felt nothing. I never talked about what happened in those places, but I wrote about them. I disagreed that reporters suffered from trauma; after all, I argued, we were the ones who got out. It was the people we left behind that suffered, that died. I did not suffer the syndromes, I did not have the shakes. I did not have psychotic tendencies. I was not an alcoholic or drug addict who needed to blot out memories. I was, I thought, perfectly fine and functioning.

Much later I met another trauma specialist in a café in London. He told me that PTSD can also appear later, long after the events. He asked me to describe all I had seen, in detail, but nothing was as painful as Luca's birth: the helplessness, my inability to protect him, and the sense that anything could and would happen. He listened carefully, wrote everything in a notebook and recorded my words, which he later sent to me in transcript form. "There are people who live in extremes," he said, "and you are one of them. You cannot think that will not affect you in some way. It has. It always will."

The birth awakened fears that had been buried. It started when I hoarded water in our kitchen: plastic packs of more than fifty bottles, which I calculated would last us twenty days. Every time I went to Monoprix to buy food, I bought more and had them delivered. I hoarded tinned food, rice, pasta—food that I remembered stored well in Sarajevo during the siege—and things that might be hard to get—medicine, vast supplies of Ciprofloxacin and codeine—which I got my confused doctor to give me prescriptions for. I hoarded bandages, gauzes, even the brown-packeted field dressings that I had saved from Chechnya which were meant to be pressed against bullet holes to staunch the blood, and I read first aid guides of how to remove bullets and shrapnel, set broken bones and survive chemical attacks. Bruno would watch, concerned but non-judgemental.

"We're in Paris," he would say, "not Grozny. Not Abidjan. We're safe."

"But how do you know? That's what people said about Yugoslavia. One day they went to the cash machines and there was no money."

I began to hide cash around the house and took copies of our passports. I made lists of what I would grab if we had to flee, and I made Bruno make an exit plan if we had to leave Paris in an instant. Where would we meet? How would we get out? I read books about people escaping from Paris after the Germans arrived, and discovered the route was through Porte d'Orléans.

Bruno finally said, "Maybe you should talk to someone about this?"

But it was all about the baby. If I was alone and caught in a terrorist attack, or a flood, or a disaster, I could manage. But I was terrified of being alone with my son if something major hit and I had to protect him. I was convinced I could kill someone who tried to harm him, and the knowledge of that darkness inside myself frightened me. Everyone on the street I saw as potentially dangerous, and when I walked down the road, I felt invisible, like a ghost, even in the brightest Paris daylight.

I knew I had to fight it. When my mother left, I began to strap the baby onto my chest with the kangaroo holder, and walk. I would start at the Place du Marché Saint Honoré, and if it was Wednesday, I went to the Italian *traiteur*, who drove his truck from Naples with fresh pasta, aubergine rollitini, *mozzarella di bufala*. I desperately wanted to feel at home, at ease, and I wanted to try to make this city—where everyone buzzed around so quickly and knocked into you with their skinny elbows—my home.

But I often felt as though I was in exile. One day I realized that war, with all its dangers, seemed utterly normal to me. My real life, my story with Bruno, was behind closed doors in some conflict zone, safe from everything else, where we created our own history. It was what I understood about him best of all: falling in love in chaos.

This real life, with all its sharp edges, was terribly difficult.

When my mother left, and when Lesley left, and when Bruno went back to work, I took the baby and wrapped him in a striped blanket, laid him carefully in his *pousette* and strapped him up, checking carefully to make sure everything was secure. Then I wheeled him down rue Saint-Honoré towards Place des Victoires.

Behind the square was a church, the Basilica of Our Lady of Victories, and here I found a haven. I went every day and sat in the back row. Sometimes I lit candles, one after the other. One for my dead father, one for my lost brothers and one to protect my baby. The baby always slept. He never cried.

The church was set on the top of a long row of stairs. To get inside the church was an ordeal that terrified me: to push the baby in his *pousette* backwards and up what seemed like a mountain. Once, in the metro, I saw a woman doing this— angling her *pousette* down the stairs that led to the train—

and she leaned back too far, and her baby slid out like a piece of fruit falling from a sack. She screamed, but the high-pitched screech of the baby that went on and on is what I remember most. People rushed forwards to check for broken bones—the baby was fine—while the mother wept. That image stayed with me for a long time.

And so we went to the safest place I knew, which was a church. Nôtre-Dame-des-Victoires was a basilica, and it was a place where the faithful had come for hundreds of years to leave their requests for Our Lady, and also to leave their notes of gratitude. I watched the Filipinos and the Africans and the Indians and the bent-over old, old French ladies praying. What did they pray for? Did they pray for sick family members, money, wandering husbands, cures to fatal diseases? I understood this. I had also prayed for a miracle—my son— and he had arrived.

Against a wall were the intentions—plaques paid for by people—and one was the story of a man, an engineer, who went deep into Siberia and was there alone for twenty years.

Pendant les vingt années d'exploration mineralogiques que j'ai passées au fond de Siberie, seul, parfois en face de la mort, et constamment en priore à d'indicibles alternatives d'espoir et de découragement, j'ai prié la Sainte-Vierge, elle a toujours daigné me venir en aide.

J-P.A (1869)

(During the twenty years of mineral exploration that I passed deep in Siberia, alone, sometimes in the face of death, constantly preyed on by insurmountable despair and discouragement, I prayed to Our Lady: she always deigned to come to my aid.)

Those days were *carême,* the season of Lent, and unlike my pious mother-in-law, Marie-Louise—known to us always as Moineau because she moved like a little sparrow—who ate a bowl of rice and nothing else on Ash Wednesday, I had given up nothing. I was not, though I believed in God and the power of the saints, a particularly good Catholic despite the years and years of schooling. But in those winter days, with my tiny baby, I was going to church sometimes two or three times a day. I made deals with God:

Please God, protect my baby. Don't let anything hurt him; don't let him die like my sister; don't let him get caught in a war or a genocide; please protect this bubble of happiness, this beautiful life. Please keep us safe. Don't let my husband die on his motorcycle.

In my pink changing bag I had endless supplies: enough to last a year rather than an afternoon excursion less than a mile from my home. Wet wipes, diapers, bottles, formula in a little plastic jar that slid open to distribute one dose, a portable changing pad, aspirin for me, a bottle of water, several sets of rosary beads, extra blankets, extra hats for the baby, my mobile phone. In the phone I had stored numbers of the SAMU, the ambulance, the paediatrician and, of course, Bruno's number.

Sometimes I felt like a fraud for the deals I made with God when I had such a cushioned privileged life. When I got home one day, I made a pact with God again, a real one. "I will give you anything," I said, reaching down to unstrap the baby, "even all the love I have in my life, even my own happiness, if you keep him safe."

In Kosovo, once, I got caught in a bombing raid. Many of the solders in my unit died. I had to live in a trench for three days, and mop up blood and bind soldiers' limbs. The commander, afraid I would report the number of dead, took away my satellite phone and refused to let me or Alex, the photographer, leave.

One day, a young Peruvian reporter who was also living at the base came to find me. Someone named Bruno had gotten the commander's satellite phone, and by chance, it was the Peruvian who picked up the phone. He had a message for me: Get out as soon as possible. You are in danger.

Somehow he had found out that I was in trouble with the commander, who was apparently going to take his revenge on me. "He said he could not say what it was," the Peruvian said, "but he stressed that you must leave."

The next day Alex and I got a ride on the back of a farmer's truck and left the base camp. When I reached the town where Bruno was, ten hours south in Albania, he hugged me tight and said he had checked the morgue every single day to see if I was dead.

I could see now, in Paris, safe on rue du 29 Juillet, how hard he was trying to keep me calm, but it was exhausting him, this role as my guardian angel. Sometimes I think, in the midst of it, he began drifting out, further and further in the world, fading out of sight, lost.

How could someone who went to wars and never felt fear when running through jungles and diving into ditches suddenly be terrified of a tiny baby?

"Darling, *you* are the boss," my mother said before she left. "He's a baby. He only weighs seven pounds."

But my fears got worse and more dramatic. They were always seemingly irrational: cities becoming besieged in a matter of hours; water being turned off; television and radio going off the air; guns, machetes, burning tyres at roadblocks.

I was sure, as sure as I was of anything, that this could happen at any time.

Where do they come from, these fears?

In April, when the spring began to come and the baby was growing sweetly, the nightmares started. Bruno's were first, and they would wake him. I would hear him in the kitchen, moving around, opening bottles, pouring wine and listening to jazz. Sometimes he woke me up with his screams.

"I can't sleep," he would say when I rose, pulled my nightgown round me and stood in the strange light that always comes in the winter between darkness and the dawn.

I am not sure what was in his nightmares, what people, what images. But my dreams were always of people, and usually the dead. People I had known who had died, people who moved in front of me, whose faces I could not see, but who I knew were ghosts. There was my father, occasionally, looking at me from some distance with profound sadness. There was my sister, still a baby, as yet unformed. Sometimes there were people I had seen with amputated limbs or bloody wounds.

"Where did you think you would die? Where was the fear the greatest?" This from the Canadian psychiatrist, examining me like a flea under a microscope. This was some time ago, and we were meeting for signs of post-traumatic stress disorder. We were in London; I was lying on a couch somewhere near Hyde Park, a couple of years before my son came into the world.

I told him about the cattle market in Abidjan, on 19 September 2002, at a time I should have been drinking my first cup of tea. But I was not. I had not changed my clothes in two days and they were stained with dirt and sweat. A government soldier stood a foot away from me with an automatic weapon pointed at my heart. It was the first days of the coup, weeks before Bruno made me leave the country.

The confrontation in the cattle market was the aftermath of a short, sporadic battle between the government forces and some mysterious rebels no one had yet seen. Like me, the soldier was confused. He didn't know who was launching the coup, or why. A superior had most likely dragged him out of bed at dawn. He was probably scared and a little drunk from drinking bad gin the night before. He stood, soaked in sweat, boots too tight, pointing an AK-47 at me and looking as if he had every intention of using it.

I wasn't alone. There was an African man near my foot, groaning in pain. There were smears of blood on his clothes and small, neat bullet wounds in his legs. A moment before, I'd squatted in the dirt and tried to drag him into my taxi. I wanted to get him to a hospital. And so, it was a showdown between me trying to take the man to the hospital, and the government soldier wanting to shoot me. The soldier said the man on the ground was a rebel, and I knew if I left him behind, he would kill him.

The soldier raised his gun, the safety catch off, and pointed it at my heart.

By the time this incident occurred, I had been reporting from war zones for a dozen years. I should have known that you don't argue with a man with a gun—particularly one who has just shot someone. The sensible thing would be to realize I had wandered into the wrong place at the wrong time—before an execution was about to take place—back up, apologize and run.

But the same dozen years had also given me the overconfidence of the survivor. And I knew what would happen if I left. The injured man, who was grabbing my ankle, pleading, "Sister, help me!" would be shot and tossed into a grave, or left with the dead cows to rot. I had never seen this man before, but I knew what his dead body would look like by lunchtime.

I squatted next to the wounded man and argued with the soldier. His impatience was turning to rage when Bruno, who was on the other side of the cattle market, suddenly spotted me and pulled me roughly by the arm away.

"This is Africa," he said. "Are you crazy?" He dragged me back to the car, silently fuming. And I was angry too; because I knew they were going to kill that man, because I had not been able to do anything, and because it was so easy and so senseless, the way people's lives were extinguished as if they meant nothing at all.

Two years earlier, in another part of West Africa, I ate a

last meal with a friend, Kurt Schork. We went to the best restaurant in Freetown, Sierra Leone, and had grilled prawns. Schork was then fifty-two, a Reuters correspondent who had been a Rhodes Scholar at Oxford with Bill Clinton. He was legendary for his bravery and his humour. During the first Christmas season in Sarajevo, which was by then besieged by the Serbs, we'd attended a midnight mass together and then drunk a bottle of black-market champagne as we listened to mortars falling on the snowy city.

Now, drinking beer in the Freetown restaurant, I told him about a group of stoned teenage soldiers called the West Side Boys that I'd encountered earlier in the day. They'd surrounded my car, punched the hood, and aimed their RPGs in my face, and demanded money, cigarettes, marijuana and sex. While my driver cried with fear, a colleague in the same car shouted at him to drive through the crowd. "Just run them down!"

"Total amateurs," Schork said of the West Side Boys. "They sound like a pick-up basketball team."

The next morning, I sat eating breakfast by the slime-green pool of our decrepit hotel with another journalist I'd known in Bosnia, Miguel Gil Moreno, the same man who would warn me of the bombs in Chechnya. It was the end of the rainy season in West Africa, and as we ate we could see dozens and dozens of frogs procreating by the edge of the water. It was like a biblical plague.

"And now," said a CNN producer, a man wearing a cravat and carrying a cigarette in a long ivory holder, "we will watch the frogs engage in sexual intercourse." He lay on the ground near the pool with a camera, filming the frogs, trying to bring some humour into the utterly grim scene outside the hotel. Miguel and I ate stale cheese sandwiches, watching; some light relief.

Miguel asked me about a home-made video I'd been given which showed men who might have been UN soldiers being tortured by rebels in Sierra Leone. It should have been a warning to both of us—look; this is the madness that happens here. But instead we said goodbye and Miguel followed Kurt and his crew up the road towards Rogbury Junction to find out if the video was real. By lunchtime both men were dead, ambushed and killed by rebels; probably stoned teenagers.

I wasn't afraid then, not as much as I should have been. There really was nothing to fear, I always told myself: it was just fate, and maybe I would live or maybe not. If you take life that way, you don't fear anything.

But I was afraid now. War is a violent teacher.

Most of all, I was desperate not to pass my nightmares, or my bad blood, on to my son.

The trauma psychiatrist, as part of his research, had once asked me: "How many dead bodies have you seen?"

I thought hard, trying to remember events and places; fields of bodies, mass graves, wells with blue corpses stuffed down them, the man in East Timor who washed up in the sewer, the slabs of dead flesh on my daily trips to the morgue in Sarajevo, the soldier in the snow in Chechnya, the miles and miles of dead Rwandans on a road near Goma. Skin stretched purple over bone. Bloated faces. How many? The fact was, I did not know. Dozens? Hundreds?

The psychiatrist was silent as he wrote in his notebook. After a while, he looked up. "Don't you find that odd?" he said, not unkindly. "Most people only see the bodies of their grandparents, or their parents, and only at their funerals."

Other than my grandmother's, my first dead body was in Bosnia. I arrived in the early autumn of 1992; it was still warm enough to get stung by a wasp, the last balmy days before a brutal winter. The war that would ruin the country was still in its early stages. I wasn't a complete ingénue—I'd been tear-gassed in the crowd during Israeli–Palestinian clashes—but Bosnia was my first war zone.

That first trip, I travelled with a nervous Australian photographer and a young Croatian interpreter down small roads that had been commandeered by various rag-tag militias. Vesna, the interpreter, gave a potted history of the former Yugoslavia and smoked all my cigarettes. We passed empty villages with shuttered houses and fields of dead animals. There were no people on the road. Through the car window came the smell of distant explosives and petrol and fire. Near Vitez we passed empty munitions factories which Vesna said had been a major industry during the Tito years.

There was another photographer in the car behind us. He was French and silent. Sometimes I drove with him. He was known to be fearless and somewhat distant, almost mystical in his intensity. Once, on a particularly spooky road, we came to a Bosnian checkpoint and I lowered my window to hand the soldier our passports. The soldier reached out, but instead of taking the passports, he stared hard at the photographer's pale face.

"What strange eyes you have, my friend," he said flatly.

The photographer frowned. "Strange?" he asked. "What do you mean, strange?"

"You have death in your eyes," the soldier said matter-of-factly. He handed back our passports, lit a cigarette and lifted the frayed rope that was the checkpoint. He motioned us through, not speaking, not smiling and not waving. The photographer was silent for the rest of the trip until we reached the car wreck. Then we saw the real dead, two of them, a couple who had been trying to flee something—fighting, a village being burned, none of us would ever know. Vesna had studied some medicine and she said they could only have been dead a few hours. *Long enough,* I remember thinking, *for their souls to fly away.*

They had driven into a tree at what must have been full speed, and they had flown through the windscreen so that their bodies lay half in, half out of the car. Their necks were broken and hung down at unnatural angles. Their eyes were still open. Their bodies fascinated me. I walked closer and stared, trying to memorize their surprised expressions caught in the exact moment of death.

That was the first real death I saw. It triggered some kind of strange autopilot mechanism in me, in which I felt very little emotion, in which I was nearly numb. Then more wars came, and I suppose an addiction grew and grew, because I got good at them, the way one gets good at a tennis game if you practise long and hard enough. When I would watch television and see a conflict gathering in some remote part of the world, I found it impossible to stay still, not to pick up the phone and ask to be sent there, and as a result I developed skills: intuition, bravery, the ability to talk or push my way into any situation, onto any helicopter or boat leaving for a dangerous place. I got used to pressure without cracking: Gellhorn's grace under pressure.

What was harder was other people's suffering. Those are the images that stuck, not the interview with the general who took out his knife and pointed at places on maps and talked about hardware and equipment. I could not bear the loneliness or physical pain of children. Perhaps that is why I feared my own child would be hurt.

The first time I saw a child crawling on a dirty cot in a field hospital with his guts ripped open and no painkillers, I went outside, leaned against a wall and threw up. But I did that only once. I learned how to observe, to write it in my notebook, and then at home, in the privacy of my room, to cry or to hold my head in my hands, to lie on the bed staring at the ceiling.

The arrogant truth was that I never thought I would die. It wasn't only me who felt this. A famous war photographer, a woman who had hidden behind a bush in Africa to photograph an execution and was renowned for her bravery, once said to me years later, "I never thought I would get killed because my mother loved me too much."

When my father was dying of cancer, I sat by his bed and we talked about many things: faith, death and war. My father emigrated from Italy to the United States as a young boy. My grandfather was an anti-fascist and the story is that they were run out of town with shot guns; I will never know what really happened because everyone I need to ask is dead. But the records do show that my grandfather, Costantino, made three voyages alone before he went back and brought his family from Naples.

My father spoke only Italian and remembers being terrified on his first day at his new American school. But he grew up to be ferociously American: an athlete, a college football player. When Pearl Harbor was bombed, he enlisted in the American air force. But war frightened him. As he lay dying, he said, "That was normal. All the men were frightened." He looked at me from his bed, barely one hundred pounds, ravaged by cancer. "I worry because you never seem afraid. That is not normal."

I went to Iraq during the invasion in 2003 for nearly five months, but even as I was packing my bag to go, I thought it would be one of my last wars. I was getting married, and I wanted a child. I knew I couldn't sustain the pace or the loneliness of those long assignments any more.

I would wander through the gardens of the Al Rashid Hotel in the early morning, waiting for the bombing of Baghdad to start, with only half my heart interested in reporting this war. I was already thinking of an escape, a life, a world with feelings and emotions and love. Later, sent to the desert with American troops, I felt no interest in the story, no excitement. A colleague who had reported wars as far back as Vietnam told me that when you lost your edge it was time to leave.

My son was born less than a year after I came home from Iraq. When I first saw him, seven weeks premature and vulnerable, it seemed impossible that I'd ever want to report a war again.

And yet when he was barely six months old I would go back to Baghdad, leaving him with his father and his nanny Raquel in Paris. Bruno told me to go. "You will understand how you want to live the rest of your life. Whether you want to continue this path or not."

I went in late summer. My breasts leaked milk and I missed my baby with a ferocity that I could not understand. I moved slowly, I could not focus, I had no interest in Sadr City or the insurgents. There was a new generation of reporters who had never been to Africa or the Balkans, and one day, trapped in an elevator with some of them, I thought: *Leave it to them.*

Dear Janine. Congratulations on your baby. You've done your bit. Now pass the baton to someone else. Enjoy your son.

This email came from a famous war photographer after the birth of Luca, when I said I would never go anywhere without him ever again. But Luca was still an infant and I was back at the al-Hamra Hotel. One afternoon I went to lunch with a famous Iraqi politician, who sat in a large empty room surrounded by his staff.

He looked at me over his spectacles. "How's Luca?" he asked. I said that he was well, at home with his father.

"There will always be other wars," he told me sternly. "But if you miss him growing up, miss his first tooth, his first step, you will regret it forever."

After nearly three weeks there, I was at Baghdad Airport and my flight home via Jordan was overbooked. There were only three seats left. A crowd of people was waiting for those seats, crushing forwards, and I surprised myself with the intensity of how I fought to get home. I shoved people out of the way, bribed someone and got the last seat. The plane took off and I looked down at Baghdad and thought: *No, I am not going to miss this life at all.* I cracked it. I ended the addiction.

And for the next five years, I watched my son, and I fed him and laughed with him and lay down with him at night to tell stories that always started with "A long, long time ago in a place far, far away . . ." My assignments were done with less passion: that passion was reserved only for my husband and my son, and the bubble of happiness that I lived in in Paris.

When I worked, I crammed what I would have done in one month into five days. I got off the plane in South Africa or India or Nairobi and I worked solidly, dreaming at night of the smell of my son's breath, milky and soft.

I did not miss my old life at all. And very slowly, the fear began to go away.

PART THREE

War is a violent teacher.

Thucydides, *reporting on the Peloponnesian wars, fifth century* BC

CHAPTER II

The First Straw

Sometime in the autumn of my second or maybe my third year in Paris, when the leaves got wet and slippery and stuck to the pavement like skin, Bruno's back broke. It did not exactly break in two like a stick, but the discs fell from their places and suddenly he had grown into an old and tired man who could not sleep and could not walk and had to lie in terrible pain for long hours on a wooden floor.

The French doctors gave him white tubes of drugs with poetic names, all opiates that dissolved in water and made him languid and glassy eyed. As one doctor began loading him up on OxyContin, I thought of my brother Richard, his eyes fired up by the morphine that he was given at the end of his life for the cancer that would eventually kill him. He was my second sibling to die.

But that was after years and years of American doctors, bored and cynical, not interested enough in patients like my brother who did not have health insurance, misdiagnosing him with an untreatable stomach condition and giving him drugs, though he begged them not to. All along, cancer was eating my brother alive, starting in his colon, his liver, his lungs and eventually working its way to his brain. But even in the days before he died, in extreme agony and wasted to the weight of a child, they would not give him the dignity of putting him in a hospice.

My brother was dying in America of a mysterious disease, and my husband's back was breaking, and I saw both of them tormented with unrelenting physical pain. Bruno withdrew with the agony. I continued to live my life as a mother, going on assignments occasionally, but with premonitions of catastrophe. I tried to push the dark thoughts back, away, to the corner of my mind, the place that housed the war memories. But Bruno was getting sicker and sicker. Most of the time when I woke up at night, he was not there in the bed next to me, and it was four or five or three in the morning, and I found him alone in the living room watching television with a full ashtray next to him. I began to feel afraid. My household, the warmth, the pink light of Paris were all fading.

But Luca grew. He was now two and a half years old, fluent in French and English, with a sweet nature. He was an easy baby who played with boats in the Tuileries, who liked to be read to, sung to, rocked. He rarely cried, did not have temper tantrums and did not mind being transported everywhere his father and I took him.

His first aeroplane flight was when he was several weeks

old, and he lay in a box provided by Air France that we strapped on the seats in front of us. Now he went back and forth to America with me three or four times a year to see his grandmother, and planes, trains, buses and taxis were as familiar to him as his toys at home. He seemed not to notice his father's withdrawal.

As autumn arrived that third year in Paris, and the leaves came down, the Tuileries grew more desolate with their black bare trees until soon there were only a few nannies walking fat babies in their strollers. The clock across the gardens on the Musée d'Orsay, which Bruno had pointed out to me with such hope for our future, seemed frosted over with the cold.

Winter came. When Luca was eight months old, for his first Christmas, Bruno took us to Strasbourg for the Christmas market. He knew I loved Christmas, loved snow, loved fir trees brushed with white, and *pain d'épices* and carols sung in incense-filled churches. But this Christmas, two years later, even while we put up the tree and hung wreaths, I felt something ominous creeping into our lives.

At 5 p.m., when I walked to the Place du Marché Sainte Honoré, it was dark. I still passed St. Roch on the way home, where we had baptized Luca when he was five months old and thrown a huge party after, and lit a candle meant to represent the scattering of light into the darkness of the world. I still stopped and lit candles when I passed St. Roch, where, in October 1795, Napoleon's batteries fired on rebels hiding inside the church. But now I did it with more trepidation.

And still, Luca grew. He wore a blue gingham snowsuit, a hand-me-down from his godmother's boy, and Raquel glued a fleece into his *pousette* so she could take him to the park for hours in the cold and come back with his cheeks bright red. As the lights got darker near the Tuileries one afternoon, I sat at my desk and took a phone call from a doctor.

"Madame Girodon," she said in a flat tone. It was someone I didn't know. She explained that she worked at Val de Grace, the military hospital known for treating Arafat and Jacques Chirac, and that she was a doctor treating my husband.

"I wanted to tell you," she said, "that I am here with your husband and I am keeping him here under orders for several weeks." When I asked why, she said it was her belief that he was exhausted and suicidal.

I held the phone and sat down in the nearest chair. I had no idea who I was talking to. All I knew was that Bruno had left the house that morning for a check-up.

The doctor was waiting for me to say something.

"I know he's not sleeping," I offered. "I know he has nightmares." I told her that he was having EMDR, a treatment for removing trauma. I began to explain what it was but she stopped me.

"I know that," she said. "I'm a doctor."

"But he's not suicidal," I said, trying to find the words. "He's just tired."

There was a lingering pause.

"May I speak with him?" I said. I heard her say something and she passed the phone to Bruno. He got on, his voice full of tears. "Do you want to stay there?" I said as gently as I could.

He said, "I'm so tired."

"All right then; stay, stay as long as you need to." I kept my voice quiet, low and calm.

"All right, baby. I'm sorry," he said.

He passed the phone to the doctor and she told me how to reach him and when I could come.

I stayed at the desk in the dark, my head in my hands, till I heard Raquel come in, her key turning in the lock, and the happy sound of Luca singing. I ran to him, pulled him from the *pousette* and pushed my warm cheek against his cold one. The baby laughed and pulled my hair. Raquel took him from me and went to the kitchen to make his pureed courgettes. I could hear her talking to him, and I sat at the desk thinking of Bruno in the hospital, alone, tired, scared. I thought of how much responsibility he had taken on, so quickly after coming back from Africa. A pregnant, demanding wife. A new city. A premature baby. "My shoulders aren't that big," I remembered him once telling me.

For so many years, people asked me about war. What was it like, did you get shot at, were you raped, how many times have you seen action, were you on front lines, what do dead bodies look like, how many dead bodies have you seen, were you scared, what do chest wounds look like, have you been shot, have you seen someone die? The more interesting ones asked: And how did it affect you?

But I was fine, I said. I did not like to talk about the places I had come back from: they went into black bound note-books and the notebooks went into a box and the box went into the basement. From there, I could look at them some-day and remember all the people, the places, the red dirt, the rain and the mud. But for now, I was fine. I always thought Bruno was too.

The trauma psychiatrist in London also said I was

resilient, and resilience had saved me. That, and being able to write it out of my system: write about being marched into the woods by Serb paramilitaries in Kosovo with a gun at my back; about the child soldiers in Africa surrounding my car with the RPG; about the dead around me. The bodies in wells, the bodies in the sewers in East Timor, the hundreds and hundreds of bodies in Goma, after the Rwandan massacre, when people—mainly Hutus—were dying in hundreds of cholera. People dropping in front of me, puking green stuff, till there was no more fluid in their bodies, then dying.

"And how many dead bodies have you seen?"

The heightened danger and ubiquitous threat that journalists confront carries significant psychological challenges. Exposure to life-threatening events creates potential risk for conditions such as post-traumatic stress disorder (PTSD), depression and substance abuse, and journalists are not immune. Data collected from a group of 218 front-line journalists who worked in zones of conflict for 15 years revealed, on average, rates of PTSD five times higher than those found in the general population. Moreover, rates of depression and alcohol abuse in this group well exceeded those found in journalists who had spent their careers far removed from the danger of distant conflicts.

—Dr. Anthony Feinstein,
PTSD and War Correspondents

So I survived, sort of. Bruno's voyage out was much harder.

I did not know how to heal my husband, and even if I had, he would not have let me.

My mother always comforted her sick children with food. It was the best way she knew of showing the love that she had. She was never one to throw her arms around you and smother you with kisses, the way I do with my son, but she was a great one for making poached eggs on toast, or farina with sprinklings of sugar, or cinnamon toast when we were home from school ill.

For this reason, I loved getting sick as a child, and perhaps psychosomatically, I was sick often, with colds, with flu, with bronchitis. I was thin and weak and pale, and my favourite moment was the morning when she would shove a thermometer under my tongue and find a fever. "OK," she would say briskly. "No school, get back into bed."

Then she would abandon whatever she had planned for her day—girlfriends, shopping, lunches. She would change the sheets, pile the bed with pillows, tell me to wash my face and teeth and fold me into the bed, pulling the sheets around me and tucking me in. Then she would bring tea with lemon and honey, orange juice and my medicine on a little dish with a spoon. It was the only time—except for in church—I remember as a child feeling that I had my mother's full attention.

She continued to pay more attention to us when we were ill even when we became adults. When my brother Richard was dying in her bed, and was always freezing cold, wrapped in layers of Patagonian fleeces and rag socks and blankets, unable to eat, and weighing about eighty pounds, she would try to feed him. She made milkshakes with extra eggs and a child's pasta—pastina—with spoonfuls of sugar. She made chicken noodle soup or grilled cheese sandwiches, none of which he could eat.

She could not address what was killing him—nor did she have solutions about what we could do. She did not know how to save him, but she could feed him. One day, she came back from his bedroom with an untouched chocolate milkshake, still frosted in the tall glass, and she was crying. "He's fading away before my eyes," she said. I remembered, as she said that, her using those same words about my father as he lay dying in the same bed ten years before.

And so, I brought Bruno food in the Paris hospital. I stopped at the open-air market near rue St. Jacques and bought half a roast chicken, some yogurt from a Greek deli, some fruit, some small lemon tarts. I bought a bottle of Perrier and some chocolate because he loved chocolate. I bought some flowers and the newspapers and some magazines. I carried all my purchases in plastic bags onto the bus which ran up past the Luxembourg, and down around the old Austrian church, Val de Grace, built by Queen Anne of Austria in 1667 to thank Our Lady for the birth of a son, Louis XIV, after twenty-three years of marriage.

The hospital nearby, with the same name, was not as lovely as the church. Inside it was sterile and smelled, like all hospitals no matter where in the world, of antiseptic and blood. The nurse directed me to the psychiatric unit and another nurse directed me to his room.

And I saw my husband. He was lying on the bed. When had he gotten so thin? When he saw me, his eyes did not quite register his wife. I put the food on the table next to him, but he barely noticed it. He was drugged up on Thorazine or something so powerful that when I looked at him, it was not his eyes and it was not his mouth or his hands. He was someone different.

He stood up to walk and a man came in, his roommate. He said hello and climbed into his bed, pulling the covers up. He was a former soldier who was, I suppose, suffering from trauma. He looked deranged. "Don't talk to him," Bruno said. "He's strange."

We walked a bit in the hallway and I met the psychiatrist. She was cold and efficient, pretty in a bland way, unemotional. I felt that she regarded me and my husband as another species. I stayed an hour, then Bruno began to fall asleep.

He came home after that, within a few weeks, but he was never really the same again, nor was our household. It was not that something had broken, but the bubble of joy, that contained little unit in which we existed, had been split in half. The ghosts of the past were chasing us. And they had managed to catch him.

On Toussaint, All Saints' Day, 1 November, we went for a picnic in the woods outside of Paris. The baby wore a fluffy striped turtleneck I had bought one freezing cold day in New York while his godmother Connie, my friend since I was four years old, pushed his stroller. Bruno had good days and bad days, and this was a good day.

He rented a car and drove us to a small auberge and we had lunch, roast chicken and frites, which I fed the baby, and then we hiked a bit, Luca on Bruno's back. We loaded the rented car with firewood from the forest, and back at rue du 29 Juillet we built a fire. Bruno lay in front of it, feline and beautiful, and stared at the flames. But when I made dinner, he would not eat.

If you were standing on our balcony, and you put your nose to the glass of the french doors, and looked in on the room inside warmed by a fire, and a mother holding an angelic-looking baby with golden curls and fat, fat cheeks, and a beautiful father, you would believe it was a perfect photograph.

But nothing is as it seems. Near the fire that night, I felt something coming, something stronger than me, running as quickly as I felt the winter coming, some kind of strange and unwanted monster, or a beast, getting closer to us, and faster, but I could not do anything to stop it. It was the catastrophe I had feared.

I listened to a song that night by a Canadian band called Stars. "When there is nothing left to burn, set yourself on fire."

Winter, and a Christmas tree bought at the Place de la Madeleine. We found it together and Bruno dragged it into a taxi and home. There were ornaments from Germany, small crystal hearts and red glass balls that I found on the rue de Richelieu, and snow from a tin that Bruno sprayed on the branches. The tree was beautiful. A friend arrived and took photos of us, black and white, the three of us, looking up at the angel on a tree. She shook her head. "You're all so photogenic," she said.

"Inside, I feel like ashes," my husband said. At night, Bruno did not sleep. He either stayed awake at his computer playing a war game called Age of Empires—"Why is it that I only like films that are either completely violent or for children?" he asked me one night—or sat on the sofa smoking and watching television.

What was he doing in those hours between dusk and dawn? I am embarrassed that I do not know, or perhaps the truth is I did not want to know, because I would find bottles the next day by the aluminium trash bin. "Did we finish two bottles of wine last night?"

"I had a couple of glasses."

He never had hangovers, but when I woke up early to see the baby or begin to work, he would stay asleep. Sometimes he slept until noon; sometimes he fell asleep on the sofa at suppertime and woke up around the time I was going to bed. He never seemed to eat. If I made him something, he would look at it reluctantly, taking bites. He did not want to go out. He did not want to see people.

But still, weak and ill, he wanted to protect us as Luca grew. When we'd been in Paris for nearly three years, we moved across the river, and he built us a house. This too was a beautiful place, an old flat by the Luxembourg Gardens; an elderly woman who had passed away left it to her children, and they sold it to us. "Hemingway lived on this street," Bruno told me. "You were meant to be here."

But the flat was ancient, it did not have modern heating,

or electricity, and it needed endless work, *travaux,* the same word in French used for giving birth, labour. Bruno found Polish builders and they pounded the walls to dust, opening up schisms of light. He uncovered the parquet floors and stood over the builder, Bogdan, while he sanded them. He chose colours that would work with the light coming from the south, special tiles from Mexico and Italy. He drove me around on his motorcycle to ironmongers on the outskirts of Paris trying to find the perfect bath stand, the perfect bathtub.

I was indifferent to all the choices, but he was like a man obsessed with building a safe house for his family. Every brick had great significance to him.

"I don't care! They all look alike!" I said of the three different claw-footed bath tubs in front of me.

"You *will* care, trust me. This is our home."

He gave himself the name Daddy Bird, because he said he felt like a bird making a nest for his family. When he set up the wireless network, he named it DADDYBIRD. He punched in his number on my telephone as DADDY.

But he drove himself to near exhaustion, and I did not understand his inability to stop, his compulsions. The more he did, the weaker I felt. It was almost as though all the independence I had was being washed out of me as the flat grew more light, more habitable. When it was over, the cupboards were brand-new, the floors shiny, the walls perfectly muted and blended colours. We organized our furniture and bought a new bed, a special one, for his bad back.

We lay on it in the Parisian department store BHV—the

store on the river famous for having every light bulb and every nail imaginable—testing it out.

"Life will be sweet in this new home," he said, and for a moment, I felt hopeful. He said, "Do you like the house I made for you?"

At home, he lit fires, ordered wood, dragged it up on his back from our *cave*—wine cellar—in the basement of our building. I asked him, restraining myself from hysteria, to be careful of his back. He seemed not to care: he almost seemed to want to break it again.

The stubborn man from the mountains, I called him, because he had grown up in the Alps. Once, when I was small, I had a dream: *You will marry a man and he will come from the mountains.* At the time, it meant nothing to me. But when I saw Bruno for the first time, when I went to the place where his ancestors came from, and where we had married, the place where he grew up, in the remote mountains near Grenoble, the Vercors, I understood him perfectly. The house had been in his family since the 1600s. The land was hilly and full of ancient trees. The rooms were enormous and cold, lit by a huge fireplace in the large room where his relatives had once cooked soup and made bread.

There was a stone fountain in front of the house that was full of mountain water which woke me on summer mornings with the sound of its softness, and on the wall in the sitting room was a chart with the height of all his ancestors as they grew bigger. The first time that I went to Grisail, the village, his father, Philippe, pulled out a pencil and ruler and measured me too.

"Now you are part of our family," he said. Luca was there, and Bruno and his two brothers growing. And now I was on the wall forever too. Because I had no real roots of my own, because my own identity and nationalities were so blurred and baffled, I loved the fact that he was so solidly entrenched in his.

The new flat was on a street called rue Notre Dame des Champs. Our Lady of the Fields. Finished, it was beautiful, perfect. The baby was growing, getting bigger in his new wooden bed with cut-out hearts that we had found in a tiny shop in the Marais: he was now too big for a crib, and tearfully I packed it up and loaded it into our new *cave*.

And at first, it seemed like things would be fine. I would cook dinner, wash the dishes and settle down. Bruno would sit by the fire for hours, poking it, making it bigger and adding to the grate.

"Are you all right?" I would ask him.

"Go to bed, baby. Everything is fine."

I pulled the duvet, white and smooth, over my nose, the way I had when I was a child and frightened that an apparition—the Virgin Mary, in particular—would appear to me. I had read too many stories about Bernadette at Lourdes.

Magazines and newspapers came to photograph the flat, to write about the life of two war correspondents who settled down and made a home. "Why Paris?" they asked.

"We wanted to feel safe."

Why was it, then, that I still did not feel safe?

"Do you think," I said to Bruno one night, "that this stuff really fucked us up for good?"

"What stuff?"

"All of it. The graves, the fires, the bombs. All of it."

He did not say anything for a while. He got another log, put it on top of the other.

"I'm the champion fire-builder," he said. "And you are the champion diaper-changer." He poured more wine.

"Did it hurt us?"

After a while, he finally answered me. "How could it not?"

He never really got to enjoy the beautiful home he had made for us. Shortly after we moved in, his back—and he—got sick again.

CHAPTER 12

Breakdown

When the body breaks down, it does not all go at once, it goes piece by piece. First it was Bruno's back—twenty years of hauling a camera, sleeping on floors and general abuse. Then it seemed his entire immune system seemed to cave in. Bouts of African malaria came back. Once, in Abidjan, he had a crisis during the *coup d'état*. It was curfew and no doctor could get to his house. So he lay in bed alone, in his sarong, sweating and freezing, sweating and freezing, with a makeshift drip hooked up to him. He says he does not remember drinking water, or eating, or getting up to go to the bathroom. Someone came and took a photograph of him which I still have somewhere—lying in a bed of sheets soaked with sweat, his fever rising, his head damp and his limbs splayed. I hated that photograph.

Once, we took a taxi together to a depressing hospital outside of Paris to check him in when he felt another bout of malaria was coming. He asked me to leave him there, to go home, to take care of the baby, because he felt that he had to do it alone. We took pictures of the two of us in a photo booth downstairs in the hospital before the nurses took him away. I am wearing a white wool hat; he is trying to make me laugh because he knows I am worried.

Then the malaria passes, and he is smoking two packs of Camel non-filters a day. He has to wear a back brace, an ugly metal and leather thing, and he is in constant, excruciating pain. Now he is not eating. Now he is really drinking heavily. Sometimes I say something. "Do you have to open another bottle? We just had one."

He lights cigarettes off the end of each other, a chain of nicotine. "Let me handle it myself."

If you read books about alcoholics, or see movies, even bad ones, that try to portray drinking, you always see a scene—cinematic almost—where the end comes crashing down. Where something gives way to something bigger. Ours came in the late summer, around the time when Paris Plages, the beach set up by the city council, draws crowds and crowds of people to the edge of the Seine. We had dinner at a Mexican restaurant in the 5th. Bruno had already been drinking, and at dinner he drank several more margaritas, more wine. Then he got on his motorcycle.

"I think maybe you shouldn't drive," I said.

He handed me my helmet. "I'm fine."

We drove along the river, the summer air hitting me in

the open place that my helmet did not cover. He drove fast. He wove in and out of cars. I wondered what would happen if the bike skidded, if we fell, if my head smashed like a melon. Luca, at home, was innocently asleep, waiting for his parents to come home uninjured.

"Slow down," I said.

"I can handle it." He sped up. He cut off a kid, a North African teenager from the *banlieue,* on a dinky scooter. The kid gave him the finger. What happened next happened fast. Bruno drew his moto right next to the kid's, dwarfing his tiny scooter. He kicked the kid's bike, and it veered slightly off the road.

"What the fuck? You could have killed him. And us." We were so close to them I could see the fear in the eyes of the kid's girlfriend, who rode behind him in a miniskirt and high-heeled boots. It was like bumper cars, but real. "God, Bruno, don't do this."

But he was at war, like when he played Age of Empires all night on his computer with various strange addicted people all over the world, and when I came in to interrupt him, he would shout, "This is war, baby!"

Then a cop was on top of us. A big cop, also North African, moustached, pissed off, aggressive. "Get down off your bike." Bruno got down. I got down. He let loose a torrent of complaints to the cop who appeared not to hear him. "Papers?" Bruno handed him his papers. "Ah," the cop said, "I see you live in the first arrondissement."

"No, the sixth. We just moved."

"The sixth, I see." Even I could read the expression on his

face: rich bastard, thinks he can kick some poor kid from the suburbs. And he lives in the 6th! The cop, after some kind of negotiation, let the North African teenager go.

Bruno exploded. He shouted back it was unfair, that the kid had cut him off, that he had been driving a moto in Paris for twenty years and knew what he was doing, that the kid was wrong, he was right.

"You're drunk, just shut up and take a ticket," I said. "If he Breathalyzes you, you're finished."

"I know what I'm doing." Suddenly I saw my husband, who had been such a heroic figure to me, as someone ferocious, angry, slightly deranged.

The cop decided he would take him to the station, back brace and all, and he could spend the night. I imagined him getting beaten by French cops, sleeping on the floor of some cell, waking up with the taste of all that tequila in his mouth.

"Good, take me to jail!" Bruno said as the cop called on his colleague for help.

I pleaded and begged. It took time. Bruno walked to the river and smoked cigarettes. "We have a baby at home; I promise this won't happen again."

The cop let us go with a huge, fat ticket. He said to me, "You look like a good person. But your husband," he looked at him, staring off into the summer river, "is in trouble."

Why do we deny ourselves reality? When is the right time to suddenly see the truth? I knew, instinctively, why I did not. It was the way that I was raised. Once, in London, my good friend Sweetie was standing by the window of my second-floor flat witnessing a crime on the street below. "Come here, come here! You've got to see this, a man just took a woman's handbag and . . ." I don't remember this, but she claims that I said, "I really don't need to see that. I would rather stay in my little world."

In my childhood world, the bad things that happened were hidden and never discussed. The sister who died was only a photograph beside my parents' bed, referred to as the most beautiful angelic baby, a child who was now in heaven. As long as my hair was brushed and my clothes were expensive, life was seemingly perfect.

But there was so much mystery. We never talked about cousins who disappeared and died, about the problems in our own home: the bags of dope stashed in the cellar; the boys' grades slipping or the fact they stopped playing sports and spent more time with bongs; the birth control pills hidden in an aspirin bottle in the bottom of my school bag; the unhappiness of my older sister and her increasing mood swings. We never talked about growing up, about what would happen when I left the painted black front gate of our home and went into the real world.

My mother made it seem that everything outside that door was dangerous and to be feared, and she kept buying me Fair Isle sweaters and plaid kilts and talking about hope chests filled with fine linens for the time I would marry.

She did not see because she could not. Her own father, Bucky, was an alcoholic who died when he was forty-eight, on his way home from work. He stopped in a bar, ordered a brandy, put his head down on the counter and died of a heart attack. But we never talked about it, his drinking, or how he died.

"Mommy . . . was he an alcoholic?"

"No, darling! An alcoholic? He had a few glasses of wine and liked to feel good."

The night of the motorcycle and the police near the Seine was the night I thought of my grandfather for the first time in many years. I knew so little about him. There were no photographs, except from my mother's wedding, and he looked young, sad and handsome.

But I wondered if he was cursed, and if he had cursed his offspring, and their offspring. I took out her wedding pictures often, and tried to find a map, a guide, by studying my grandfather, who had died more than twenty-five years before I was born. In the tinted photographs, he guides my radiant mother down the aisle in her satin 1940s dress that was so beautiful it was given to a historical society as an example of the lines from the fashion of the period.

Theirs was a wartime wedding, and my father wore his air force uniform. There is a row of bridesmaids in tiered satin gowns and pretty little girls in long skirts and braids. The photographer got drunk at the reception after and passed out, so there aren't any more photographs other than those two. Later, when my father came home on leave, they had to repeat the pictures, but my mother was already pregnant with my sister and could not zip up the dress. "I could have cried," she always said. "My wedding day."

"What did Bucky drink?"

"Wine, very good wine, and brandy. Sometimes Scotch."

My brother Richard drank Scotch too, but he had been in rehab five times by the time he died at forty-seven, and he was proud of the fact that he was sober for ten years. Alcoholics Anonymous got him sober, and he carried, like most AA devotees, the little blue book which has inspirations to help keep them sober. But even after ten years of not drinking, he still called himself an addict. "If it's not one thing, it's another," he said, and told me that people became addicted to AA meetings as a way of replacing the drink, the longing for oblivion.

Before he died, Richard's addiction became painkillers, but I understood so well his vortex, the darkness of the pain that he was suffering. I understood it well because I had the same: not physical, but my addiction was to disappear into the world, and often a dangerous world where there were no rules.

"It's in the genes," Richard told me. "Bad blood. Crazy, Gerard blood." Gerard was my mother's family—a family of surgeons, lawyers, chemists and senators. They were, my mother had always told me, "a good family." We used to joke about the crazy blood, inbred from years of the Gerards marrying second and third cousins.

But despite their sometimes misplaced snobbery, some of them ended their lives alone and miserable. One, a distinguished doctor, disappeared on the streets of Manhattan. Another, a musician, was murdered in his apartment in Miami. Another died, aged thirty-two, of cirrhosis of the liver, alone in Arizona. And Richard died of lung cancer, alone one autumn night, not far from the Shrewsbury, a river in Red Bank, New Jersey, that leads to the sea, in the same hospital in which my father had died ten years before.

The doctor who tended him at the end would not give my brother a painkiller to fight the extraordinary pain that must have been racking his body. In fact, he said had too many opiates in his body and gave him an injection of a drug that reversed the painkilling effect. So Richard's last hours were spent in terrible distress, struggling to breathe.

The doctor would not let my sister Judy, who had tended my brother with devotion all of his life, into the room. He made her wait in the hall with my other brother, Joseph. They waited for hours, and my sister kept watching Richard through the window of his locked door. He was half hanging off the bed, struggling, nearly unconscious. She went to sit in the hallway, distraught, helpless, waiting, and constantly checking him through the window. But she could not touch his hand, or comfort him.

After several hours a nurse came running to get her. "Hurry! You have very little time."

She and Joe arrived just in time to each hold his hand. He turned to her. "I waited for you," he said. Then he died.

When they came to tell my mother that Richard was dead, I was in France. They say she curled up in a ball on the floor, in the position of an infant in the womb. When I heard that, all I could think of was my mother losing two children she had given birth to, two children leaving the world before her.

I cannot bear to think of my brother's death. I try to console myself that he is in a better place, that he was so lost in the world, that he found something much better. For my sister, it is worse. She is haunted by the fact that his final hours were alone and in pain, even though she had promised him he would not die alone. We tried, in the beginning, to bring the thick medical files to doctors, to find what had gone wrong so that his life had been so horribly lost and ended in such a violent and brutal way. Judy wrote endless letters that never got answered, and confronted doctors who gave her cold, contrived answers. Eventually, she gave up.

Two days before he died, I had called him in the hospital. His voice was so faint. My brother, the coolest, most handsome boy in town, the best athlete, the smartest, the fastest, and the older brother all my friends had a crush on. The one who listened to Jimi Hendrix and Crosby, Stills, Nash & Young and the Allman Brothers Band. The one who had parties when my parents were in Jamaica or the mountains, with wonderful and strange people with Afros and caftans and tie-dyed clothes coming through the door, while I lay upstairs in my bed with my Raggedy Ann dolls.

"Take care of your little boy," he said. Those were the last words he spoke to me. *Take care of your little boy.* Because, I suppose, no one had taken care of him, not the way he needed, not the way he should have been.

I was in Grisail, Bruno's mountain home, when I last spoke to my brother. Over the miles, I wished him with all my heart some peace going into the next world. *Take care of your little boy.* I remember how I ran off into the forest after that call, and cried my heart out for the little boy who was so beautiful, so haunted and so misunderstood, and whose life was such an unbelievable waste. *Take care of your little boy.* Bruno followed me into the woods. He did not say a word, just took my hand and led me to special places in the forest on his land. A small space where the trees parted. The bridge where Germans shot his ancestors a few days before the war ended, and where two wooden crosses marked their graves. The small altar to Our Lady, across the cow pastures, where we had walked the day of our marriage to lay a bouquet of pale pink roses at her feet. *Protect our marriage and our little family,* I had prayed.

Even now, I cover the pain of my brother's death with something harder, a shell, a belief that it's easier for me to live in a world where I get slightly more of my mother's attention because my brother is not around to suck up all the care. "Your brother is going into rehab again," I remember my mother saying. I was seventeen and needed her attention. But she was exhausted. "I don't have time for this now, darling," she said. She sat on the stairs in our old house, the big house we had all grown up in, now long sold, long gone, and cried. I can't remember what I needed her for. But it was forgotten. I sat next to her on the stairs and stroked her arm.

So my brother was lost, and my husband was lost, and I was determined of one thing, more than anything else in the world: my son would never be lost.

The relationship one has with drugs or alcohol or whatever it is that takes you into another realm—addiction—is something I struggled to understand. I had tried everything in my life, but nothing ever caught me in its grip. I could smoke a pack of cigarettes under stress, then not smoke again for a year. I could drink, but if I did not drink ever again, I would not miss it. I did not think I was addicted to the adrenalin that seemed to affect other people when it came to reporting war. But two of my brothers struggled with addiction, and I was beginning to see that Bruno's addictions were similar. He was unable to do anything in a small way. Everything he did, from falling in love, to building a house, to having a baby, was done with tremendous attention and all his energy until he was depleted, emotionally and physically. He could not have one glass of wine; he had to have the bottle. He could not just fall in love and marry; it had to be the greatest love story in the world. He could not have a child without being the one to do night shifts for a year, feeding the baby, being the protector of the household, until exhausting himself to the point of no return with his unending love and sense of responsibility to his family. So he cracked.

I was too young, or perhaps never wanted to see it, to understand my brother Richard's rehabs. One day he was home, the next, my mother would be sitting at the kitchen table in tears, and he was gone. I had no idea how long he stayed, what he was doing, who his sponsors where. I knew he had a sponsor at AA, and that in many ways he saw the programme as his saviour, something that rescued him from drowning. But he also met his nemesis at one of the meetings, a woman who got him hooked on the prescription pills that later played a part, I believe, in killing him.

Once, a few years after Richard died and when I was at the darkest point of the struggle with Bruno's addictions, I found a diary of my brother's from rehab. I was home visiting my mother and someone had accidentally put it in the old oak bookshelves that had been in my childhood room. It was a journal of my brother's recovery and the twelve steps, and at the end, his friends from rehab had written their comments. Most of them were alike. Words of simple encouragement: *Stay sober; stay clear.*

God, thank you for keeping me straight today and help me stay straight tomorrow.

At the end of the diary, I found one written from someone called John: *Rich. This is your fourth rehab. You know what to do. If you don't this will be your last, and you will be dead. Good luck. Your friend.*

After Richard died, I called J., a writer friend in Paris who was heavily involved in AA, whom I had met at a dinner and who had explained to me his own voyage into addictions, drugs, alcohol, and how he had eventually woken up so ill in a hospital that there was nothing else to do but get sober.

I remember the night I met him, because Bruno had been with me at the dinner, sitting across from me, miserable, unhappiness etched on his face, drinking more and more wine and looking utterly alienated from the people around him.

Bruno went home early, and J. walked me home along the river. It was a hot night, July, and tourists passed us in their awkward shorts, holding maps. "I think," I told J., "that Bruno has a drinking problem."

He was thoughtful. He said that he could help, but only when Bruno came to him, only when he was ready. "No one arrives at the point where they are sober," he said, "until they are ready."

So, a few days after the motorcycle kick, and the police and the Seine and the Mexican restaurant and the tequila, I found J.'s number and rang him.

He did not seem surprised to hear from me. "I need—we need—help," I said.

"I'm here," he answered.

Bruno went away again. He came back from a work trip to Spain gutted. "I'm tired," he said, crawling into bed, pulling the sheets over his head.

The second rehab was a place in the country with bars on the windows. It was more a detox centre than anything else: at night, Bruno went to the sitting room and Skyped me. His face was white, hollow and thin. He was not allowed visitors. I called his mother to tell her he was in the hospital, yet she did not seem aware of the gravity of the situation. Moineau did not, could not, understand. "Yes, he told me he was very tired. It's a rest, isn't it?"

I thought of my own mother, unable to see when her own son was drifting further out to sea. Perhaps we protect ourselves from ourselves.

My husband and I talked over the internet, and I placed my hand on the screen, trying to touch the harshness of his face. I felt unbearable sorrow at my inability to help him.

How long had I been in love with him? And why, I wondered, had I fallen in love with someone who was so distinctly disturbed? So fragile?

"*Ça va?*" he said hollowly.

"*Ça va.* And you? Are you sleeping? Eating?"

He looked away. He was smoking. He said there were bars on the window of his room.

When he came out a few weeks later, we went together to see a woman named Irene. She was French, but had lived in America for many years; she had a strange, Woody Allen–style New York–Jewish accent, but entwined with French inflections. She was in her sixties and beautiful: her grey hair was pulled back in a chignon and she wore no make-up on her strong face.

As far as I could see, Irene had several articles of clothing, all impeccably cut, which she alternated: a black straight skirt, a perfect white blouse, a black crew-neck cashmere sweater and a pair of plain fitted black trousers. She wore neat pumps in the winter, without socks, and a pair of Greek-fisherman sandals in the summer. Her feet were beautiful, her unadorned toenails shone like smooth rocks.

She was calm.

We sat in three chairs, like the three little bears, and she said little, but watched us. I cried, Bruno smoked, Bruno cried, I smoked. Irene would listen and then she would say, "We must stop."

Outside, we climbed on the motorcycle and drove home, passing Trocadéro, passing the river, going by the Ferris wheel where he had carried me over the threshold in the millennium year. There's a photograph of it somewhere: happy people, in love. Then we probably went and had a drink.

Bruno said one night over a glass in a café near Irene's house: "I saw the Ferris wheel going up, and I thought, I have to take my wife there—it's been so long since we did something fun."

"It's OK. You're not well."

When we got home, he put his helmet on the shelf and went into a darkened room to sit and watch television. When I went in to say goodnight, he said, "I'm so sorry. I'm lost. I've been lost for a very long time."

CHAPTER 13

New Identities

In time, I grew to alternately resent and hate AA because in some ways it stole my husband from me. He stopped going out at night or socializing with anyone who was not a member. He went to meetings at least once a day, sometimes twice. The only person he spoke to, aside from me, was his sponsor. I knew it was keeping him sober, but I was not sure, as someone had told me, that it was not one addiction replacing another.

I went to a meeting, and listened to people talk about their worst moments—hating themselves, waking up in gutters, pissing themselves, blowing up toilets, ruining marriages and lives. Grudgingly, I went to Al Anon—for family members of alcoholics. I did not think I needed it, and left halfway through when the members started arguing about who was making the tea. I read the twelve steps. I read books on co-dependency. I began, as best as I could, to detach.

But Bruno says he really stopped drinking because of Luca. One day, the two of them went to the shop across the road, a place run by Algerian immigrants, where we buy milk when we run out, and vegetables, or fruit. Luca looked at the high shelf, the bottles of dark wine, pointed and said, "Daddy." After that, Bruno had one more drink—on my birthday—lapsing from the sobriety about a year after he stopped drinking. He opened the bottle of wine that we had saved from our beautiful wedding in the Alps, the idyllic day during the canicule with Luca nestled in my belly, and me in a white dress, smiling at the sky, smiling at everyone.

We had married on the Feast of St. Amour, 9 August, because we believed, and we told each other, ours was a love story blessed by fate: it was simply meant to be; no matter how hard we tried to run from it, it had caught us both. We were destined to be together. The wine we drank that day was a special Beaujolais, a gift from Bruno's brother Patrick, also called St. Amour. We had cases and cases in the *cave,* enough for a lifetime of opening a bottle on birthdays or Christmases, or our anniversary, and remembering, with the slightly woody taste of the wine, why we had married that day.

It was the saddest birthday, the day of his last drink. Not because I grieved for the passing of his alcoholism, but because I knew, instinctively, that he would change and never again be the man I married. Because, in fact, part of that love was based on the passion, the drink, the fury, the rage, the anger, the drive, that made him so intense. Without it, there was a smaller person who looked sad and hardened by life.

He opened the wine. My mother-in-law brought out a lamb casserole she had baked in the oven all day, and the house smelled of beautiful spices from Provence. Bruno toasted, "To my wife," and gave me a long white silk dress that wrapped and wrapped and wrapped around my body with metres of soft gauze. Then he drank a glass of St. Amour, said it was his last ever and went to bed.

I sat up with my French family, drinking a home-made digestif brewed from herbs that came from the mountains not far from our home, but all of us were aware there was someone missing. When I went to our room, I saw Bruno curled in a ball, sleeping fitfully in the big wooden bed that had belonged to his great-grandfather.

He shouted in his sleep, he cracked his bones, he tossed, turned, like someone absolutely miserable in his own skin. He was, I decided, a wounded animal, a tiger or a lion. Eventually, he gave up trying to sleep at all. Near dawn, I heard someone outside, and I could see him, standing near the basin of spring water that came from the mountain above the house, staring into the grey light at nothing.

February has always been a hard month, a seemingly long month, a grey month. The exception was the year Luca was born. That year, one cold day passed into another so swiftly and I woke with my fears, but I woke joyfully, rushing to the baby's crib to scoop him up. I was cocooned in happiness.

That year, even February, with its impossibly dark mornings, its chill and fevers and hacking coughs and early, depressing dusk, had some joy.

Four years after our wedding and three years after Luca's birth Bruno tried to go sober. The first February of Bruno's recovery, when he went to an AA meeting every day and isolated himself from everyone and everything in an effort to reconstruct himself, something also happened to me. The cocoon of my family life opened a crack, and I walked into France for the first time.

In the early years in France, Bruno protected me from everything. He told me that Saint Bruno, after whom he was named, meant shield. He shielded me emotionally and physically, from his alcoholism, from bad things happening, but he also protected me from the complexities of French bureaucracy: the dossiers; the long lines at the *mairie* to present various folders of papers; the telephone company; the complicated social security. Even the army of Polish builders at our new apartment were off-limits to me. "I can do it," he'd say when I would show up to help.

It was true that he was, as he described himself, a control freak, but it was also true that I had willingly given away all of my power. I had wanted to. I arrived in France fragile, pregnant, somewhat broken. It was the first time in my life, since I was very small, that someone else took care of me.

I thought briefly of my Italian grandmother, Antoinette, who arrived in America when she was forty with four children. My grandfather, Costantino, was authoritarian and stubborn: he spoke English, and had his own business, but she must have been terrified enrolling her children in school and shopping for food in a language that was not her own. He wrote the cheques and paid the bills. She stayed in the kitchen, or saw her enormous extended family, all of whom also spoke Italian.

Even though a similar arrangement could be made in Paris for me—there is a parallel world that exists for Anglophones that includes schools, doctors, tax services and lawyers—I suddenly realized that I was going to stay in Paris, and I had to become a part of it. My tiny world of my husband and my son, keeping us insular and safe, had to open.

I had stubbornly, for some time, tried to hold on to my identity because I had fought so hard to create one—was I an American of Italian origin, as Bruno described me, was I British, which was my nationality and described the place I had passed all of my adult life, or was I now French, which meant I belonged, in some ways, to my husband and his culture, and not to my own?

One day, I dreamed in French, which was the beginning, really, of my life in France. Luca's school was a French one, and there was also Alice, who helped me. Alice wore leather trousers and silver necklaces with tiny jangly butterflies, had a small dog named Clive and a cat named Louis. She lived in a garret in the 7th, off the rue de Sèvres, six flights up, no elevator. She spoke English like a character out of Agatha Christie, but she was French born and bred, as were her parents. Her grandparents had been British bohemians who arrived in Paris in the 1920s, lived in Montparnasse and collected art, but she had not really learned English properly until she went to a British boarding school. She was obsessed with grammar, in any language.

I went to Alice to learn how to write properly in French—to master the impossible tenses like the *passé simple* and the *futur antérieur* that I had learned in college and then promptly forgotten, because soon I would be doing my son's homework with him. And Alice loved tenses. She thrived on precision, she cringed if I used the *passé composé* instead of the *imparfait.* She told me the thing she hated more than anything was when people used the subjunctive badly. She hated hearing people speak French and make mistakes. She also hated it when English was not used properly, and she used grammatical terms I had not heard since the third grade, when the nuns had used pointers to break down sentences. She winced if I used slang I had picked up from Bruno.

She loved punctuation and homework and exercise drills. She said my French, which had served me fine for five years, had horrific grammatical mistakes. She said miserably, "I wish you were a *débutante.* Now I'm going to have to undo all of your bad habits."

Bruno had told me the mistakes were endearing, my accent was sexy, and not to worry about grammar. His English was fluent—learned from Clint Eastwood movies and working in Anglophone countries. When I asked him about the *passé simple,* he shrugged: "Don't worry about it."

When I explained this to Alice, she frowned. She looked slightly wobbly. "This is terrible," she said. "Grammar is *so* important." She produced an enormous book of grammar, the kind I had studied when I was fourteen, and said that I had to memorize every noun and its gender. "There are more than three thousand," she said solemnly. "And there is no way around it other than to memorize every one and know which is masculine and which is feminine. That's the way it's done in French schools, and that's the way your son is going to do it."

Meanwhile, my son spoke French at school and French with everyone but me. To me, he spoke English, and when I asked him a question in French, he ignored me. I once heard him explain to a shopkeeper, *"Ma maman est en train d'apprendre Français"*—my mama is in the process of learning French. I have friends who have "mixed" parents, and they have always told me how mortified they were to hear their mothers open their mouths to speak French with strong New York accents. So I did this weekly *supplice* with Alice partially for Luca. A victory was doing *devoirs* with him as he was sounding out letters, and him giving me the thumbs-up: "Mama! You said it perfectly."

Twice a week, I climbed up Alice's crooked stairway. I dragged the heavy book back and forth, often cursing it, and did my *devoirs*—my homework—which was usually a written essay, while lying in bed. It had been a long time since I had studied, done homework, or drills with someone pointing a pencil at me, someone getting annoyed when I made a mistake with complex verb tenses. But it was for that reason— I did not want Alice's displeasure—that I kept on going. And I read the newspapers every day in French, and bought novels by Louis Aragon and poems by Baudelaire and struggled at night with Proust, then gave up and bought the English versions. And I knew, somehow, that this was all about self-improvement and independence from Bruno, about breaking out of my bubble.

We did endless *dictées,* where Alice read from complicated art magazines and I copied down her words; we had conversations about the difficulties of mothers or men, but mostly we studied grammar. It was mind-achingly boring, but somehow strangely satisfying, like going on a stringent diet and seeing the results.

Through Alice, I felt that somehow I had made my peace with France. I remembered going to the Monoprix with the Mary Poppins nanny in the earliest days of Luca's arrival, Luca strapped to my chest in his kangaroo carrier, and literally freezing in terror of the rows and rows of dairy products: What was the difference between *fromage frais, fromage blanc* and *faisselle?* Was *crème legere* sour cream or whipping cream? What kind of butter did I need when there were twenty different varieties: salted, unsalted, some for baking, some for cooking? And why couldn't I find the pasta I had always used, the mozzarella, why couldn't I find a pizza in Paris that was not made by Tunisians?

I chastised myself, because I had shopped in these kind of places all over the world and managed: factory-sized Jordanian supermarkets to buy supplies for Baghdad, with rows and rows of food identified in Arabic; crowded and noisy Jakarta food markets to bring tinned tuna and juice cartons and vitamins to East Timor; under-stocked outdoor stalls in Zagreb during the war to bring siege food to Sarajevo. That was fine.

This, the act of feeding my family and having to do it in another culture, was—like the birth—daunting.

My friends at Monoprix, the people who comforted me with their soft smiles and their own stories of homesickness, were the Sri Lankan cashiers who told me about their families and how they missed the wild landscape of their country, and how to choose the best and cheapest apples by the kilo. And later, I would come and see them crying when the tsunami hit, and they could not reach their brothers, their sisters, their mothers. I identified with these sad and lonely and lost women, not the chic French women in tight trousers holding a near-empty basket with a few slices of jambon, a bottle of Badoit, and a pot of yogurt.

Alice also taught me other things that my mother-in-law or Bruno did not: after a man riding a bicycle on a pavement nearly knocked me off my feet then shouted *"Dégages!"* at me, she told me to give it back to the French in the same manner they gave it to me. She told me to not allow shopkeepers at Le Bon Marché, the elegant Parisian department store, to get away with insolence. She said it was her personal mission to do battle with every single Parisian shopkeeper or waiter who had bad manners (this seemed completely pointless to me, but never mind), and she taught me exactly how to do it. She told me where to buy cheap bath mats and how to bargain for prices; she told me stories of her girlfriends' online dating adventures; she told me about the difficulty of French men. "Never go near," she once said sternly, "any man who dyes his hair." She told me where to go to get the best skin cream in Paris for the best price, and gave me the name of a dermatologist. Soon the sessions were more like going to a shrink, but in French, and with the occasional correction of the *passé composé*.

The second wave of relenting to French life was to learn how to cook French food. This I resisted for the longest time. Even though I felt I was now liberated by being able to curse in French at shopkeepers or people who deliberately tried to run me over with their bicycles on the rue de Rennes, I felt I would lose that identity—whatever it was—if I started cooking like my mother-in-law, with all those *rognons au riz* or *pot au feu*.

I resisted selfishly even when Bruno—who never complained, who ate everything I cooked, when he did eat— occasionally spoke longingly of his mother's *mousse au chocolat,* which she heroically produced by the basinful at our wedding, and which was gone in an instant, along with the foie gras she made from scratch, painstakingly picking out the veins of the goose liver.

I would resist when we were on holidays in the mountains in Grisail; when she tried to show me how to debone a lamb shank or make a flourless chocolate cake, I would feign boredom. I daydreamed when she and Monique, her glamorous best friend, who had long blonde hair well into her sixties and looked like another Brigitte Bardot, took me to the organic vegetable nursery and bartered over courgettes and peppers and pumpkins, and showed me how to pick the best ones, and how to make confit and jams and pastries.

I rolled my eyes in boredom when she talked to me about the wonder of Picard, the French frozen food market that is beloved by French cooks because everything is so beautifully done and packaged, and because you can serve *coquilles St. Jacques* at a dinner party and no one would know you had not cooked it yourself. "This is how easy it is to puree leeks," she said, washing the stalks one by one in a basin of cold water.

My resistance to making a *daube* or a *tarte aux pommes* was also something to do with lingering homesickness, being in exile. When I cooked, it was the food that came from my family: risottos, pasta and chocolate chip cookies for Christmas, Easter eggs dyed red, like the Greeks did, in April. When I went out, I did not want foie gras. I craved food I never used to eat. Cheeseburgers, for instance, or turkey sandwiches. Once, I saw an American friend who had lived in France for many years walking down the rue Princesse smiling to herself. She had just come from a Parisian coffee shop renowned for serving American-style food. "I just ate a tuna fish sandwich," she said in a dreamy voice. "And my entire life in New York City flashed before my eyes."

While I was pregnant, in the isolation wing of the hospital, and then after Luca was born, all I wanted to eat were tuna fish sandwiches, which are not easy to find in Paris. Bruno would bring them to me, but they weren't the crustless kind on white bread that you got in an American deli—they came on baguettes with lettuce and sliced egg. And so, for these reasons, trying to maintain my own piece of America, I dug my heels in firmly and refused to learn to cook French.

Eventually, I found the only Italian restaurant that did

not use Tunisians as cooks, and another place thirty minutes away on the metro that had real mozzarella. I paid outrageous prices for a jar of Skippy peanut butter, and when people came from America, I made them bring me Pepperidge Farm Goldfish and Arm & Hammer baking soda instead of trying to abandon my cravings and eat what the French ate—*rognons,* snails, oysters, quivering foie gras (the fresh kind, cooked with apples and served slightly raw), *tarte au saumon* and macaroons from Pierre Hermé on rue Bonaparte that people loved but that I thought tasted of fish.

My yearnings were satisfied by less satisfactory equivalents of what I desired. So the pizza I finally found after five years searching in the 18th arrondissement was not ever going to be the Neapolitan pizza that you eat at long tables and that is as thin as air. And the Anglo-style bakery Bread and Roses on rue de Fleurus, which served Earl Grey tea and a very good carrot cake, was lovely, but it was not Tom's in Notting Hill, which served pink fairy cakes and ginger cookies and fried eggs and ham. And the waitresses in Bread and Roses, who charged seven euros for a glass of iced tea, were charmingly pretty but extraordinarily rude. "Yes, seven euros for iced tea, and what of it?"

One day, like the resistance to speaking the language with the proper grammar, I gave all this up. I was in France. Why was I fighting my internal battles through the cuisine? I went to London at least once a month and could eat curry and chilli squid there. Also, there was Moineau.

Moineau did not have daughters—Bruno was sandwiched between an older and younger brother—and she always treated me like the daughter she never had. The first time I met her, she opened a bottle of champagne and kept the bottle, always, on a kitchen shelf in Grisail. She gave me a sapphire and diamond pendant when Bruno and I were together for a year, which her father had given her. When things grew difficult with Bruno, she would phone me, to make sure I was all right.

But my memories of my mother-in-law will always be about food. The first meal she made for me in Grisail was like eating a burst of sunshine: it was a tagine of lamb and aubergine in a tomato sauce that she had baked for hours in the oven, and a *citron tarte* for dessert. At our wedding in Grisail, our lunch was roast lamb, gratinée potatoes and a *pièce montée*—the traditional cake for weddings, births, baptisms and communions, made from small circles of glazed hardened sugar, stuffed inside with cream and towering in a triangle: an act of love.

The day after the wedding was Bruno's birthday. Moineau cooked the picnic lunch: prawns, foie gras and her flourless chocolate cake. At Luca's birthday parties, she did not make the American Duncan Hines cakes with frosting; she arrived with elegant creations that came in small boxes and were as neat and perfect as she was. When she picked Luca up after school—the tradition is that French grandparents come once a week to collect their *petit-fils*—she arrived with a white cardboard box tied with a pink ribbon and inside was one perfect, nearly warm caramel éclair. I knew that Luca would grow with this memory of food, of his grandmother at the door of his little school, with something sweet and delicious and loving for him to eat. She even got him to eat pureed leeks. And it was Moineau who had fed him his first bite of solid food when he was three months old, a spoonful of carrots with crème fraiche.

And slowly, very slowly, I fell in love with France.

I once read somewhere that French women have the most difficult job on earth, the job of being perfect in every way, and that they consume more antidepressants than any nation on earth. When I look at Moineau I understand the enormous pressure these women feel, which is perhaps unique in the world because there is such an emphasis on perfection. Now I understood why the midwife had been so scornful of the sugar I had eaten while pregnant; I had gained more than twenty kilos while carrying Luca. The competition in France for women is fierce.

Moineau is tiny and beautiful. She had three boys, but like Monique, she still looked like Brigitte Bardot: a tiny upturned nose, a blonde bob, elegant clothes. When I saw photographs of her holding Bruno as a two-week-old baby she is already back at her pre-pregnancy weight and wearing a tight sheath, her hair and lipstick perfect.

She told me that it broke her heart to go back to work when her boys were small, but she had to, and so she hired a teenage nanny. But she ran home from her job during her lunch break so that she could prepare a perfect dinner for her husband and sons. She worked full-time, plus ran the household, plus reconstructed the family *mas* at Grisail.

Her early life was about order and perfection, but even as she grew older, she still maintained her rules: she always seemed to be on a diet—something about respecting the rules of time of eating—and lectured me about eating only 70 per cent dark chocolate (the best brand, she advised, being Lindt).

Before dinner, she usually drank a glass of whisky, which she called a *"petit apéro."* She and my father-in-law, Philippe, who was as handsome as my husband, and had served as a mountain guide on skis during his military service, were a couple that remained in love until he died snorkeling in Tahiti while they were there together in March 2011. They were a grand Catholic family, and loyalty was everything.

She made her own jams from strawberries and raspberries in the summer, and in the winter knitted all of Luca's sweaters and my hats and scarves. She knew how to find the best price for good handbags or shoes. She smelled, like my own mother, of expensive perfume, of Guerlain.

There was nothing, I was convinced, that she could not do.

She had told me over and over, for the first five years I was in France: "You must cook French food," and she would regard my pastas and roast chickens with slight suspicion. One Sunday, she had enough. She arrived at my house with a basket. It was, she said, a cooking lesson.

The night before, I had read *La Bonne Cuisine Pour Tous (d'apres les vieux préceptes de la grandmère Catherine Giron),* stained with red wine and gravy from past Girodon cooks, a book which I had found in the kitchen at the house in the mountains. And the Christmas before, she had given Bruno a notebook with all her own recipes, handwritten, pasted with flowers, painstakingly listing all the ingredients in her careful looped penmanship.

It was nearly springtime when we started the cooking lessons, so she wanted to do veal. *"Le menu,"* she announced, unpacking her gear, *"c'est blanquette de veau, du riz et tarte au citron . . ."*

On Saturday, she phoned and told me to buy *"une tranche de jarret de veau"* (a slice of leg of veal) for each person, plus carrots, lemons, crème fraiche, butter and sugar. She would bring the cooking wine and the handmade bouquet garni.

On Sunday mornings, there is a famous market on the Boulevard Raspail outside my front door. They sell beautiful, if overpriced, fruits, vegetables, meats as well as cheese from Normandy, fish from the coast and organic breads. I used to love the Sunday ritual: the little orange trolley on wheels I bought because everyone else has one; the flirtation with the man who sells organic baguettes; the long-haired American hippy who makes raisin cookies; the hot chocolate that is sold halfway down the market; and the towers of fresh lemons, oranges and apples.

But now it's a recession and the market is double-priced and I worry about money. So the veal comes from a less pricey butcher on the rue du Cherche-Midi, an old man who takes forever to cut the meat, and whose wife counts the change and asks about my son and whether or not he would like a *steak haché.*

The lemons come from the Arab grocer across the street,

who also knows Luca and who gives me a thumbs-up early on school mornings as he is raising the awning and I am holding Luca by the hand, and who always gives me overripe bananas for free to make banana bread.

Moineau arrived early, having gone to mass the night before; Philippe, she said, was at the morning mass. She asked for a cup of chestnut leaf tisane, and unloaded her *batterie de cuisine,* placing each item delicately on my counter: a tiny steel instrument to make lemon zest and a minute whisk. The bouquet garni was made from fresh thyme, parsley and rosemary.

She looked appalled at the state of my knives, but my best casserole, which was a gift from a French friend, seemed to mollify her. She melted oil and butter and put her ear to it to listen to it bubble. Then she added water, white wine, carrots—she does not use chopping boards, finds them boring, instead she cuts while holding her hand upright:—"It's how my mother taught me, *c'est comme ça*"—and chopped some small onions from Chez Picard.

She left it for two hours and turned her attention to the *tarte au citron.* She peeled two lemons in her hand, using the twist of a knife, and leaving behind a beautiful curl of yellow skin, which she told me to throw into the fire that night as it would make the room smell good. The naked lemons went into the blender with sugar and egg white. She put the yolk of the egg into a small cup for the veal sauce.

She then taught me to make rice the correct way. While waiting for it to boil, she made me a rose blossom tisane and showed me exactly how many teaspoons of rose petals to put in the pot. The tea went into fragile china cups that belonged to my grandmother and were shipped across the Atlantic from Italy to America, then back across the Atlantic to England, then across the Channel to France.

She told me news about Monique, her best friend, and about her brother, J.P., and how worried she was about Philippe since he fell from a ladder the summer before fixing something in the house. She spoke sadly about the pained relationship with her own mother, Mamie (whom we had buried five years before, on a rainy April day, my birthday), but how beautifully Mamie sewed and how she made Moineau a white dress for her graduation. She told me how much she loved her father, a judge in the naval court. She told me about growing up in Morocco and Senegal under French colonial rule, and about how much she loves her husband, whom she met when she was twelve. She told me about studying economics, about her favourite professors. About films she loves, always romantic ones, or ones that make her cry.

Then, after the tisane, while we were still talking and while the sky was growing darker with oncoming rain, the meal was ready and everything happened at once. The veal was spooned into a thick white bowl. The rice was buttered. My father-in-law, whom we call Bapu, arrived late from morning mass, and Bruno and Luca brought me flowers.

We laid the table with six handpainted plates that came from our Lyonnais ancestors, a wedding gift from a snobbish cousin called Jean-Louis, now dead. We opened the wine— Moineau wondered if Bruno would mind; in fact, he did not, or tried not to: he often opens wine himself and sniffs it and pours it for everyone else, the test of his endurance—and we sliced the baguette at the last minute to make sure it stayed fresh. Bruno, who never seemed to eat in those days, only smoked, for once sat at the table with us, and we lifted Luca into his Swedish chair, which grew along with him because it had little slots that we moved down as he grew so his feet didn't touch the bottom. I took the cheese, a brebis from Corsica, from the fridge to soften, and sat between my son and my husband. My mother-in-law seemed happy, content. She took small bites and did not complain. We ate the veal, followed by the cheese and salad, followed by the lemon tart, which tasted of spring. The language at the table was French.

It seemed, for a short while, that this was a perfect little family again, that nothing bad would happen, and that for the moment, even if it was short, a respite from reality even if it was just a Sunday afternoon, and the rains were coming, it was an impasse, everything was all right. I tried to hold that to me, to believe, against everything, that my intuition, which always had served me, which had kept me alive for so long, was wrong and that something bad was not going to happen after all.

PART FOUR

Choose something like a star

Robert Frost

CHAPTER 14

Finding a Place

The Sunday before Ascension—the French holiday that breaks the month of May in two and heralds the beginning of the summer season—the chicken man in the organic market on Boulevard Raspail gave me a free *demi-poulet*. It was not, as I saw it, simply the fact that I had gotten an extra two breasts and two wings of a chicken: it was a major and significant turning point of my life in France.

Every book I had ever read about earnest foreigners in magical Paris always included a generous shopkeeper: the butcher who gave extra bits of meat for their dog; the kindly baker who dropped another *pain aux raisin* into their bag for their toddler; a *legume* seller who took ten minutes to explain how to make a fresh artichoke salad. I had the Algerian fruit seller who gave me bananas, but the magical food world of

Paris, the generosity of Parisians, had never really touched me. When I would go to Nicolas, the wine merchant on the rue du Cherche-Midi, and ask for a wine to go with our dinner of lamb or fish, I never got a lecture on the difference between Burgundy and Bordeaux, which I wanted and hoped to get. Instead, in a perfunctory way, the shopkeeper picked a bottle from the shelf and rang it up.

"Eighteen euros. *Merci.*"

There were no friendly lessons from the cheese vendor, either, trying to sort through the four hundred varieties of French cheese at the beautiful but overcrowded cheese shop Quatrehomme on rue de Sèvres. Someday, I thought, I would buy a book that would explain the difference between goat's cheese and sheep's cheese and when to serve each, and the seasonal changes of cheese, but I knew it would probably sit on my bedside table like *Paris for Kids: 68 Great Things to Do Together.* But the Sunday before Ascension, the day before Luca was due to leave for his first *classe decouverte*—nature class trip—I decided I wanted to go to the Sunday market to buy a roast chicken.

I was with a friend who was visiting from Afghanistan. It had been raining for two weeks in Paris, sometimes gentle rain, sometimes thundering tropical storms that reminded me of Africa. He wanted to see the market and we went early. That morning, the sky was turning from grey to blue and back to steel. It was drizzling as I wheeled my orange basket down the street and stopped at the first stall to begin to pile it with vegetables. At the chicken stall, the man who cooked the chickens on a spit and drove up from the countryside each Sunday, asked me how many adults and how many children I was having for lunch.

"We're a lot," I said. "But just give me one big chicken."

He looked perplexed. "You won't have enough to eat."

"We're fine. It's plenty," I said.

I could see him thinking, weighing something out, and when he loaded my chicken into a paper sack, and poured hot juice over it, he also piled extra breasts, wings, and legs.

"You should feed your guests properly," he said. "People like to eat on Sunday." He charged me nineteen euros, the price for one roast chicken, though he had given me nearly double that. He handed me the sack and said I was *très jolie,* and why shouldn't I have more chicken when I had such a lovely smile?

I smiled again, for the man was close to seventy, and he was not being lecherous, he was being kind. I put the waxy sack into my trolley and smiled all the way through the crowded market, with people shaking drops of water off their umbrellas and Japanese tourists taking photographs of piles of rhubarb. It was a small victory, completely insignificant in the scale of the other things going on in my life, but the extra chicken for lunch made me infinitely happy.

Luca was five years old, in his first year of real school, *école maternelle,* when he went away on his first school trip alone for two nights. I was not happy about it. But the ethos of his school, l'Ècole Alsacienne, founded in the 1850s by French Protestants, was autonomy. Children were meant to be independent as early as possible. They were meant to be able to put on their little coats by laying them on the floor, then threading their arms inside, then flicking them over their heads. The first time I saw Luca do that, shortly after he started at the school, I was amazed. Where had my son learned that?

I had been preparing myself to say goodbye to him for a long time and I had known about this trip long before he started school. It was part of the school's philosophy, one that I had previously regarded as brutal. Separate children from their parents? A New York friend had been the only one in his class not to let his nine-year-old go to Brussels for a week. He took his son, instead, on a trip back to the United States to see relatives. "Nine is too young to be alone for a week in a foreign country," he insisted, and I agreed with him. But Bruno, being French, did not.

"That kid will be stigmatized by being the only one in his class not to go," he said. "It's a bonding exercise."

Luca's bonding time came fast, and the school and the parents were prepared. A psychologist was brought out one evening, to answer all our questions. The director of the farm where the children would go and live for the few days came and explained how the doors locked from the inside and how each child slept with another friend with a hole in the wall for adult supervision.

Leaflets were distributed weeks in advance with instructions for packing, for writing letters to our five-year-olds that would be read to them while apart from us, so it would not be dramatic when it came to saying goodbye.

A few weeks before, perhaps sensing my own nervousness, Luca began to say he did not want to go. Bruno warned me not to talk too much about it as a separation, but as an extended time to play with his friends.

"It's going to be fun," I told him half-heartedly, remembering going to camp for the first time, being separated from my mother, and waking up in the middle of the night crying. And I was twice his age at the time. "It will be great."

"Mama, I don't want to go to the big house," he told me, because we had seen pictures of the large castle-like building where he would be staying. And to Bruno, he said he did not want to go because Stephanie, his teacher, had told them they would give themselves showers, but would not be able to wash their hair.

"That's because Mama will wash it before you go," Bruno said practically. "And I'll wash it when you get back." Luca seemed unconvinced. The morning of the trip, Bruno woke me at six-thirty. "Wake him gently," he said. "And don't make it a big deal. It's like any other day."

I had packed Luca's clothes the week before in my own little red wheeled suitcase and I had added the special label with his name the school had given me. I had, for the sake of my son, followed instructions carefully, something that went against the grain for me. "Follow the list!" the teachers had lectured us. "Don't put extras in the suitcase!" For once, I was not rebellious.

I had written two letters to Luca which would be given to him at mealtimes, saying how much we loved him, how proud we were. I had packed his Thomas the Tank Engine backpack with "one snack, one small bottle of water, one *doudou*—a stuffed animal—and one game."

At 7 a.m., I carried my sleepy son, who still had his round baby cheeks, reddened by the impression of his pillow, and smelling like lavender soap, to the sofa in the living room. As I passed the hall mirror, I saw myself with Luca, whose legs were now so long that they hung down to my knees when I carried him. His size shocked me. In my mind, he was still a baby, but his size, his language, his actions—he was, after all, going to spend two nights alone with his classmates in a forest outside of Paris!—told me my little boy was growing up, very fast, and very sweetly.

I wrapped him in the striped blanket, a larger version of the one I had swaddled him in when he was an infant. I laid him on the sofa. He closed his eyes and smiled, moving his face towards the sunlight coming from the east, from the Luxembourg Gardens. I made him lemon crepes with brown sugar and fresh orange juice. I picked out a red Spiderman vitamin, bought in America, and carried it to the low table by the sofa, the one Bruno had bought in Indonesia.

I cuddled my son in my arms, fighting anguish, and he woke up and began to talk about a lemonade stand that he would build in the summer. This was one of the few bits of Americana I had instilled in him: Thanksgiving, a song I had learned as a child called "Over the River and Through the Woods," and lemonade stands and blueberry pie from Maine. I fed him the crepes, and in between bites, he said how he would build the lemonade stand:

"You take scotch tape and put up a sign. Then you mix

lemon with sugar and water, but . . ."—he leaned his mouth towards my ear—"it's a secret recipe. Then like Bugs and Daffy on Baby Looney Tunes, you build a desk and sell the lemonade for one cent. You put your piggy bank on the desk and people put money in. One cent."

"You can charge more than that, sweetie," I said.

"Five euros?"

"Twenty cents is fine. And you can give them a free cookie with it."

"Yeah! Anna's cookies." Anna was his American au pair, who made peanut butter and sugar cookies and played American games with him like Mother May I? and hopscotch.

"Anna's cookies," I said.

But as he was dressing, he became a baby again. "Mama, I don't want to go to the big house," he said, shivering slightly.

"It's OK, it's going to be fun," I said, unconvinced.

Bruno brought a bag from the bakery across the street: warm croissants and *pain au chocolat,* and he and his only son lay on the floor together. I watched their faces, so much alike, and I wondered why Bruno did not seem to feel the sharp pain I did that Luca's babyhood was finished. He would tell me, often and solidly, when I spoke of how hard it was to let the days on rue du 29 Juillet go, "They were beautiful days, and these are beautiful days. Don't grip on to things. Let them go and other things come."

Many years ago, in Maine, Marc, who would become my first and very young husband, before I had begun reporting war, when I was still a student who wanted to grow up and become a professor or a novelist, had said to me when I complained that I remembered so little, "You're not hanging on to enough of the moment."

This is the moment, I thought, looking at them both. *Remember it.* Remember the details, the colour, the smell. Remember the sound of Luca talking quietly, whispering to his father in French. His baby teeth, still shiny, not yet lost. Remember the faint light coming through the windows. The smell of the sugared crepes, the colour of the orange juice I had squeezed for him.

"Let's go," Bruno said suddenly, rising from the floor. "It's time. The bus leaves at nine sharp." Luca and I looked at each other. I saw in his face the softness of a child, but also something else: a slight defiance, the emerging of an individual. He was half Bruno and half me, for sure, but he was also very much Luca Girodon.

They took the motorcycle, Luca in his new red helmet, and I walked along rue Notre Dame des Champs, pulling his suitcase to the meeting point at La Closerie des Lilas, where long ago Hemingway was usually found getting drunk with his friends. *A shot of brandy,* I thought, *would make me feel better now,* and I briefly thought of the old Bruno, the fun one, the one who ran down the length of a bar in Nairobi while the barman tried to catch him, just so that he could lean down and kiss me passionately.

"That was the most romantic thing I have ever seen in my life!" my Kenyan friend, Anna, had said. Her husband, Tonio, was there, too. Tonio and Bruno were doing shots at one end of the bar, there were pretty hookers from Somalia everywhere, and soon a fight broke out, and we got kicked out. Then Anna and Tonio had a fight, and Tonio ran off, and Bruno went after him; then Bruno and I went to sleep while Anna and Tonio kept fighting. There was a crash in the middle of the night—Tonio had broken through a wall of glass. Bruno rushed down to try to calm things. Everyone went back to bed. In the morning, there was the pure, hot Kenyan light and the smell of coffee. We were due to fly to Samburu land, but Bruno woke and said he had to go back to France; he was too disturbed, too *"perturbé"* by the scene the night before. He drove to the airport and changed his ticket while I stood in shock, but remained stoic.

"When will we meet again?" I said.

He shrugged. "I don't know, but we will."

This was us. No map, no rules.

There were crazy nights, and even crazier resolutions. The most romantic thing I ever saw. The most romantic man I ever knew. But now we were parents, Bruno was sober and the intensity of those days was exhausting us. We wanted peace. We did not want the ghosts around us any more.

Bruno always told me the reason he loved me, the reason he married me when he had always said he never would marry anyone, was that no matter how much it hurt, I always let him go where he wanted to when he needed to, when he had to. It was not about other people, about other women, other places. It was about his need to be alone, to be free, to be unencumbered.

"Go if you have to go," I said, and kissed his cheek. His eyes filled with tears. I knew he loved me. I knew no one could ever replace me. What else mattered?

I knew there were others like me with complicated

spouses. Simone de Beauvoir once said it about Sartre and his hundreds of flirtations: "Once you know there is something irreplaceable between you and another person, nothing else matters." This was the way our relationship went—in and out, back and forth, two steps forwards and three back.

Before Luca, it was our life. That day in Africa, Bruno flew back to France, we broke up again, we got back together again, we lived continents apart, we reunited in a wave of passion, we stood in front of a priest and took our vows, we made a little boy, we became parents.

Then Bruno broke down, a carjacker in Nairobi killed Tonio, Anna got married again to a Samburu warrior, and Bruno and I tried to live the best we could with the brutality of our history, sometimes scratching out the pain and with a compulsion to be better, but always trying—at least we felt—to be honest.

At the meeting point, we loaded Luca's red suitcase onto the bus. I gave his teacher, Stephanie, the two letters I had written. I had drawn hearts over them in yellow ("Mama, what is your favourite colour? Mine is yellow because it is happy. It is the sun!") and red and green ("Green for Christmas, yellow for summer, right, Mama?"). Bruno and I went for a coffee at the café on rue d'Assas, and I ate a tartine and read *Le Figaro*, trying to take my mind off my anxiety.

Bruno drank an espresso silently, smoked two filter-less Camels, then pecked me on the top of my head and went off on an assignment, "To the suburbs, the rough neighbourhoods." It struck me that for the first time in five years, we were alone without our son. Even though we sometimes went away together for the weekend, in the old days, before AA, while Moineau and Bapu watched Luca, this was different: our son had left us, not the other way around.

"Do you want to go to a movie tonight? Or hear some jazz? It's the St.-Germain Jazz Festival," I said. Bruno loved jazz. He had listened to it endlessly all those long but wonderful nights when he stayed up with the infant Luca.

My wounded, fragile, impossible husband frowned. His beautiful face, creased with pain that I could not read. "I have my meeting tonight at eight-fifteen. It's about the Big Book."

The Big Book, the bible of AA. The meetings at the American Church, Quai d'Orsay. Right next to the Musée d'Orsay that I had stood and looked at from my balcony at rue du 29 Juillet, the huge illuminated clock at the top of the building, feeling such hope and happiness. Now I hated passing that church. I hated the smell of the rooms where AA held their meetings. It was the alien spaceship that had opened its doors and taken away my husband.

But this was selfish, I know. Because AA, of course, had saved him.

I smiled. "Don't worry," I said. I was not disappointed. This was a version of me in Kenya, saying goodbye; me in Los Angeles after a passionate two weeks together when the final night consisted of us both crying because we could not give each other what we wanted (me, a baby; Bruno, the ultimate freedom); me in Jalalabad, saying goodbye to him forever.

I was saying goodbye again; I was exhausted by the comings and goings. And Bruno hated long goodbyes. He called it "red eye blinking eye" because when he took a photograph of the two of us in Los Angeles airport after that particularly painful break-up, I had been crying for hours and he was rapidly blinking back tears. When I boarded the plane—in those pre-9/11 days, when your companion could accompany you all the way to the gate—I turned around to see him blinking over and over, tears falling down his cheeks. How long was it after that I did not see him? I lost count. Once it was weeks, another time months. I would try to put him from my mind, but it would always be impossible to forget each other, to find a replacement. We would always reunite somewhere with the ferocity of firecrackers. We found each other again in airports, in war zones, in cities.

And he would always save me. Me running in the door after a brutal bombing in Kosovo, wearing a funny wool hat a soldier had given me, and Bruno playing poker with some of his TV colleagues in a seedy hotel in Northern Albania. He put down his card and dragged me by the hand outside. "Such joy!" he said, seeing my dirty, bedraggled face. Me in Afghanistan, after months and months travelling with the Northern Alliance towards Kabul, sleeping in tents, sleeping on the ground with bronchitis so severe it hurt to breathe, and Bruno sending with a colleague antibiotics and a warm nightgown that he had bought at Princesse Tam Tam, a shop I loved on rue Bonaparte. Then our meeting, in Jalalabad, months later, him kissing my face over and over.

"Did you miss me?"

"What do you think?"

Him in Burma, undercover, filming child labourers, me in Sierra Leone, two of my friends murdered, hiding secret papers linking the government to blood diamonds. Bruno on a Burmese train, opening his washbag and finding a small bottle of my perfume he always kept. "And I opened it, and I wished I had not," he wrote to me later, "because all of the memories came flooding back." Our meeting in Paris: me running up the seven flights to his apartment, him opening the door with a huge smile.

After Grozny: "You're alive. I told you that you would be alive."

After East Timor: "What happened there?" Then a pause. "You don't have to tell me if you don't want to."

Our days in bed, sleeping together, getting up only to buy food at a Greek delicatessen and take it to the Chateau de Vincennes on a summer day, lying on a blanket and listening to jazz.

And the meeting after months and months apart when he was in Africa, fighting his demons, the war waging outside his door, and me at home growing bigger and bigger with his baby; opening the door to my London flat, and there was my new husband. I threw my arms around him, and buried my face in his neck. We would never ever be apart again, I vowed. Neither one of us would ever be in danger again.

I had wanted, he had wanted, so desperately a clean life.

So much joy, Bruno had given me. And today, the middle of May, there was other joy. Our son was growing, Bruno was not drinking, and I was leaving, finally, the sadness of the past behind. And out of this chaos, there was a child. After him, perhaps there would be more children, Luca's own someday. Marguerite, Bruno's Hungarian acupuncturist, a woman he called "my angel," had said when Luca was born: "Now you and Janine are immortal." It was no longer us. Our time, in a sense, had finished, together or not, but that little boy forever bound us. And I knew, even if I never saw Bruno again, or if it was years before I saw him, I would never have nothing to say to him. He would always be the person who spoke the same language as me.

My husband rode off on his motorcycle down rue d'Assas, smiling behind his new helmet, driving to the suburbs to work, and I finished my tartine and read the day-old news in the *Herald Tribune,* while Luca, on the school bus headed to Burgundy, rolled off to his first adventure.

CHAPTER 15

A Tentative Peace

Il faut en profiter. Enjoy it. Enjoy him. Those earliest days, when Luca was wrapped in his soft white rabbit suit and I was holding him tightly to my chest, everyone told me how fast it went. How short their infancy, their childhood. Enjoy it. Watch him. Take the images and freeze them in your mind. *Sage comme une image.* A baby as good as gold.

People warned me that children grow up and they don't need you any more. I could not possibly believe this. My son had been premature and unable to dress or feed himself; we had had to clean the stub of his umbilical cord. It seemed inconceivable that one day he would play on the floor without me, surrounded by Lego, or that he would even say, "Mama, close the door. I want to be alone."

I had wanted, perhaps in a kind of rebellion against my

early periphrastic life, to be a wife and mother, that 1950s kind, who makes her own pastry and wears a stick-out skirt. I wanted to be a good wife, to try to administer to a sick and wounded husband. I had tried, but ultimately, as Martha Gellhorn once said to me, talking about some dictator, a leopard does not change its spots. And when Luca was nearly six years old, I went to Afghanistan.

It was not a long trip, not long by my old standards when I'd be away for months and months; and it was not a trip that involved heavy drinking or wild flirtations or wonderful passionate nights falling back into bed with someone who spoke the same disoriented language of war as me. But it was certainly a trip that changed me. I had vowed, even written publicly, that I would never put myself in danger again. And while Kabul hardly seemed dangerous to me after Chechnya or Liberia, there were kidnappings. A security guard who came to pick me up to bring me to the airport was appalled at my guest house. "Do you feel safe here?" he said, checking the roof. "Anyone could get in." He told me the guard at the gate was stoned and useless and that I was totally vulnerable to kidnapping and attack.

"I'm OK," I said. The fear that had gripped me in Luca's early days was gone. I did not feel as numb as I had during my most reckless period, but there was something of the old spirit that had returned. After that, I went to Cairo. On the flight back, we sat on the runway for an hour. I put on my dark glasses and tears rolled down my cheeks as Bruno sent me text messages about love, about redemption. About Luca.

Bruno left for Pakistan. He had not drunk in more than

two years. He went to his meetings. He shaved his head, something he had once done before when he was in the midst of a dark period. He saw few people aside from Luca, to whom he was the most wonderful and loving father, and me. But when he spoke, it was in AA talk. His life was centred on the work he did inside the walls of the church at Quai d'Orsay.

There were times when I wanted the bond that we had, the promise he made to me that night in Sarajevo years before, to end. "I will never lose you." Sometimes, in frustrated and bitter moments, I had ugly thoughts: I wondered if it would be better if his plane went down in the Indian Ocean, or if the Taliban in Waziristan kidnapped him because then the union we had, the beautiful union, would be frozen forever in time, and would not change so drastically.

I knew, in a sense, we would never be free of each other. Even if I chose a different life, a healthy one, one that was not tainted by war or illness or breakdown or even Paris, I would always have him in my life: he had vowed he would never lose me. And there was also our son.

Bruno always had the ability to read my mind, to know me sometimes better than I knew myself, and he sent me a note one evening on my telephone: "The promise I made to you in Sarajevo will always remain. I will never lose you."

But we were separating. We could no longer live together, not as a couple, not as the two people who had brought the baby home from the hospital and built fires in rue du 29 Juillet or who had ridden the Ferris wheel in the Tuileries or taken off for weeks on the back of his motorcycle. He had changed and so had I.

One night, late, an SMS arrived from an old, old friend, another woman reporter I had met in Sarajevo. Karen was a beautiful woman with whom I had many shared memories, and we had a friend in common, a character, a strange and troubled man, a reporter who had fallen off the radar after the Bosnian War.

Karen's message was short: *Marchand finally killed himself.*

It was nearly midnight when I got the message, and I got out of bed. I wanted a drink, but there was no alcohol in the house. I wanted to smoke, and I searched in my desk drawer for an old cigarette. I could see Paul Marchand's face: his smirk, his strange cruelty but also his humour. I called Bruno in the small studio where he used to stay while he was in recovery, in rehab, as he called it. And where he now lived.

"Paul Marchand hanged himself."

"Holy fuck."

"It could have been you. It could have been me."

"It wasn't us. Go to bed, baby. You're alive."

But I could not sleep. I lay on my pillow with tears running down my face, trying to call my friend Ariane, who had come back from five years in Afghanistan wounded from living for too long in violence, and who now lived around the corner. "I'm tired of living around guns," she said. I had shared an office with her in Sarajevo, and she had first introduced me to Paul. "I know," she said sadly, when I told her. "I feel like I'm surrounded by death."

I remembered things I had forgotten long before: escaping from the besieged city for forty-eight hours to meet

Bruno in Germany, and not telling my office. Returning to Sarajevo, and seeing Marchand. His joking, teasing. "Hey Janine, your editor called and I told him you left your post to go meet your boyfriend." How he shared his food, his cans of Gini orange soda that he brought into the city by the caseload.

He had apparently been a beaten child, the child of alcoholics who abused him. None of us ever knew that. He stuttered as a small boy and had been bullied at school. We only saw a tall, rather handsome man with a city coat and shiny shoes who seemed reckless and crazy and addicted to war. Who stupidly drove around a city that was targeted by snipers with the words on the side of his car: *Don't waste your bullets, I am immortal.* Who then famously got shot and severely injured, losing part of his arm.

But there was a gentleness to him, too. One time, shortly after I first arrived in Sarajevo, I was not able to wash because there was no water, and I remember sitting in his room while he patiently heated a can of water and helped me wash my hair, then dried it by hand. "Now you are beautiful!" he said.

Another time he rang my room at 2 a.m. "The water is running and she is hot!" It was December 1992, and for a rare hour the electricity worked in the Holiday Inn, Sarajevo. There was water coming out of the creaking pipes. The toilets flushed! The telephone rang!

Or the time we found the old people frozen to death in their home near the front line, and his outrage, his indignation: "We are going to the UN and telling them to take away the bodies. Or we put them in my car and we do it ourselves."

Kurt Schork was there too; he was dead, now Marchand. And Juan Carlos, a Bolivian journalist who always made me laugh, who had shot himself after he said he saw too much. The last time I saw him was 5 a.m. at my apartment in London, after a long drinking session.

"I won't see you for a long, long time," he said, walking down the stairs.

"What do you mean? I'll see you soon."

"No. It's time." I knew then what he meant. "I've lived enough, seen enough, and drunk enough. It's time." He died too.

The years had rolled on, and I had married that strange man who fell on his knees in front of me in Sarajevo. My father died. My brother died. I became a wife and a mother. "You are alive and they are not," Bruno had told me.

No one tells you when you give birth about the real sadness of parenthood—that children grow up. The baby who smiled at you, and stared in your eyes with undying love, looks at you and says, "Mama, please don't talk—I am thinking."

The man you marry, who stood before you in church, or in a registry office, who held your hand when you gave birth, and kissed your forehead with such unbridled tenderness, also changes. People who deeply love each other cannot always live together; this is the real sadness of life.

Eventually I slept, but the old nightmares came back, and in the morning I wondered if they would ever go away.

. . .

"Your French passport is here." Bruno calls me while I am in the souk in Cairo. In the background is the call of the muezzin, a sullen and melancholy sound that will forever remind me of my early twenties and Jerusalem, before I became a mother, before I became his wife.

"You're now officially French. Congratulations, baby. I'm so proud of you." Then softer: "But I have always been proud of you. No matter what you do, I am always proud of who you are, and what you are." His voice was full of sorrow.

I thought briefly of all we had done, all we had gone through—the war, Africa, the coup, his back, the drink, the cigarettes, the fax from Kurdistan. All the love letters, and that very first, left by my window in Sarajevo: *I won't lose you.*

Then the desire for Luca; all those miscarriages, the loss, the tears, the sorrow, the bitterness, the eventual triumph when he was born and Bruno called out, "He has your hands!" The hand-knitted jumpers, the ruffled white blouses like Pierrot; the trips on Air France in a little box, the first day of school, the rolling adventure. Our life in Paris.

And that summer, for the very first time, our son learned to swim. At Ascension, we went to St. Barts, the place we had taken him when he was three months old—in those infant days he slept on two chairs pushed together—and he waddled out into the pool without floaters, and he swam, one arm in front of the other. "Mama! Look! Look!"

I picked up my passport at the St. Sulpice police station, alone one late summer morning, careful to get there in plenty of time before the window slammed shut and all the officials went to lunch. Bruno had wanted to come with me,

to film it, but he was in Pakistan at the time, and besides, I
felt there was something important about me going alone. A
moral victory, of sorts.

I dressed carefully, respectfully, and walked to St. Sulpice,
taking the long way down rue d'Assas. I felt like a bride,
fresh, arriving somewhere for the first time.

I made it to the police station, and spoke my careful
French to the person on the information desk and found the
right office, a maze of French bureaucracy, but this time, my
stomach did not get in a knot, and the French words came
easily to me. The man behind the desk who took my receipt
was rude and unpleasant—typical of French officials—but
like millions of Parisians, I did not react. Who cares what he
thought, how he frowned as he searched through the piles of
burgundy passports till he found my complicated name, how
he barked at me to put my right hand on the biometric
meter. I had my passport. I was French. He did not congrat-
ulate me, and I did not sing "La Marseillaise," as I had
expected. I put it in my bag and held the door for an African
woman wheeling a *pousette* into the room. I hoped she was
picking up her passport too.

I walked outside and it was a bright shiny morning. I
wandered through Bruno's favourite park, the tiny triangle of
green across from the Hungarian Cultural Centre on rue
Bonaparte, and cut through the Luxembourg Gardens. It
was that time of year between the end of summer and the
beginning of autumn and the trees were full and still green,
but I could see the first chestnuts of the year falling on the
dusty pathways. There were some children playing in the

sandbox; my son had loved that sandbox but now he was too big—he said it was for babies.

I wished, on some level, that Bruno could have been with me and he could drink a glass of champagne at the Café Vavin, where once we had celebrated my birthday with bottles of it; and where once, years before, I had a sore throat and he ordered me a hot whisky; and where we had broken up, tearfully, again, one winter day after the war in Chechnya. I knew he would never be able to drink champagne with me again, that the bubbly, early, frantic and crazy days were over.

But it was all right. I sat on a bench and examined my new passport, wished myself well. I had done it. I had gotten through the tears and trauma and I had lived through a dozen wars, even though some of my friends had not. Bruno was still alive and had not killed himself on his motorcycle, or with drink, or with his gun.

From the other side of the park, I saw Luca coming towards me, wearing a pair of red corduroys and a beige jumper, skipping, holding Anna's hand. He was happy, his smile as big as a pumpkin. "MAMA!" he shouted. He let go of Anna's hand and raced to me. I scooped him up, and held him as close as I could. He would always be mine, even when he grew, even when he no longer needed me. "Look what you made," my friend Roy, now also dead, had said to me the first time he saw him, when I opened the door with the baby in my arms. *Look what you made!*

I pulled Luca tighter to me, and waited for the next big thing to happen.

CHAPTER 16

Endings and Beginnings

For two years in a row there was snow in the Luxembourg
Gardens after New Year's Day. There was ice on the duck
pond, the fountains were frozen, snow piled outside the
gates. The runners in their winter layers of Gore-Tex and
wool skidded and glided, and used the exterior of the park to
run rather than slip and fall on the narrow paths. Luca and I
spent a Sunday climbing on the roped-off, forbidden areas of
the Luxembourg, making snowballs.

Outside, in the real world, there was a crisis. The financial
markets had collapsed. Across Eastern Europe, the gas pipe-
lines had been turned off. Babies in maternity wards in Bul-
garia were freezing: nurses warmed their tiny clothes on
space heaters. One year, as I planned Luca's fifth birthday,
nine hundred people died in Gaza in an Israeli offensive.

Had I not been baking his chocolate birthday cake and preparing for eighteen children to come and hit a piñata with a stick, I would have been there. Possibly.

There was a freeze around Europe, and Paris looked more like Moscow to me, with hanging icicles and dark mornings, than France. But the news of the world—Gaza, Kabul, Baghdad—still seemed far from me, wrapped in the warmth of my living room on rue Notre Dame des Champs, watching Baby Looney Tunes dubbed in French alone with my son. "*Sacré bleu!*" said a tiny duck wearing a diaper. I had never actually heard anyone say that except a duck in a French cartoon. Then the spring came, the summer when Luca perfectd his swimming in Greece with his godfather, and when I was beginning to get used to taking him on holidays by myself and fielding questions from people who said, "Where's your husband? How is he?"

One day, walking down the street holding Luca's hand, I realized, the way you realize when the sun comes through a thick woolly cloud, that I was no longer afraid. Perhaps it was because my son was older, and I knew he would no longer stick his fingers into electrical sockets, or that I could tell him to be careful of cars, and not to go off with strangers, but suddenly the metallic fear that seemed to travel with me everywhere since his birth was gone. In its place were a lightness, a joy, and a habitable place where I could raise him without thinking about backyard wars in the Balkans or Africa where neighbours turned on neighbours with machetes or guns. I was like everyone else. At a party, I met a psychiatrist who told me about how trauma can occur—

something happens in your past, lies dormant, then is re-activated by an event. So Bruno's trauma came with the wars because something must have happened to him earlier, a wound unhealed.

I belived I had escaped trauma because I passed the wars unharmed, I thought, psychologically. But the birth of my son opened up receptacles of recall, of memory, of those wars. I was not as unbroken as I had thought.

Bruno's demons remained. He continued not to drink, but it was, I could see, a daily battle; it took huge courage. He missed the taste of alcohol, and the padding it gave him from the reality and sharpness of life. He insisted, in a macho way, on opening bottles of wine for guests—he would sniff the cork and the wine, then pour. "You don't have to do that. No one here wants to drink," I said one Sunday when I had prepared lunch for three friends, none of whom were drink-ing. Bruno had run down to the corner shop and brought back a bottle of Bordeaux. He poured two glasses, one for a friend, one for me, even after we both said we did not want it. Later, when he went to his meeting, I poured the wine down the drain and took the empty bottle to the bin in the courtyard.

And now another year had passed. Soon, Luca would turn six. I knew that I had to return to the world. Partly because Bruno had actively left it, or at least left the world we had built together.

After our separation, he had taken a room around the cor-ner in the 15th arrondissement. The apartment on the Lux-embourg Gardens that he called his nest, that he built by hand for Luca and I, no longer held his energy.

We rebuilt our lives. He bought a futon and used the blue Kenzo sheets that were on his bed in the Marais when I first met him, half a million years before. We still loved each other. I realized there would never be a day when I would not love him fiercely. But neither one of us could really function together in a world that was real, as committed to each other as we were, and to our son. Life, with its sharp edges and complications, did not work for us as well as we worked together in wars.

Outside, people were still living. When I looked out of my windows to my neighbours across the street, the rooms were lit up, and there were festive dinner parties. The Christmas holidays were approaching, and even through the gloom of the recession, people were drinking champagne and good wine. Bruno went, sometimes, to two AA meetings a day to get through the holidays.

There was not much money, and the papers talked of the worst job and financial crisis since 1945. So I shopped carefully: one jar of honey from the Raspail market instead of two or three. I tried not to think of what we had done the years before: engraved Christmas cards, champagne, caviar dinners at Dominique, the oldest Russian restaurant in Paris, now closed, and presents of La Perla silk lingerie from rue Faubourg Saint-Honoré. Possessions had never meant much to me. What I had wanted, more than clothes or cars or books, was security. I wanted to feel safe. I wanted not to be lost in the world.

Twice, just before the holidays started, we had gone alone to eastern France, to Alsace. Bruno knew I loved Christmas, that it reminded me of the happiest times of my childhood:

my father driving us home from my Italian grandfather's Christmas Eve dinners and listening to a reindeer report on the AM radio. My Italian aunts and my mother spending days making seven fishes for the Christmas Eve meal. The church scented with pine, the way the children's choir sounded when they sang "Silent Night." My entire family, still alive, and all young and healthy, sitting around a long walnut table draped with my great-grandmother's handmade lace tablecloths and no one fighting. Limoges china and a crystal vase, too heavy to lift, a wedding present to Grandma Buccino in 1916 that held lemon-scented water in the centre of the table. The taste of the special cakes, the bowl of walnuts with the heavy silver cracker. My father's face. My brothers and sisters. My mother.

One Christmas with Bruno had been golden, the first year of Luca's birth. It had been one of the first trips we took alone without our baby. For a few days at the beginning of the Christmas season, we left him with Raquel and his grandparents, and Bruno found a small inn outside of Strasbourg. There was snow on the ground, and we huddled inside. When we did go out to the Christmas markets, we drank mulled wine and ate things that came in juniper or cinnamon sauces, and walked through snow and down small streets that led to canals.

He took me to a holy place, a stone monastery perched on a crag of a rock. The legend was that a princess had fallen in love with a man against the wishes of her family, and something terrible had happened, and so the family had built the chapel in her memory. There was a church called the Chapelle des Anges—Chapel of the Angels.

"Look," Bruno said, "it's our son." Pictures of winged babies, cherubim with fat face and hands, painted on the frescoes.

We sat in churches and listened to organ music. We ate *choucroute*. We bought *pain d'épice* made into the shape of hearts and had everyone's name engraved on it in white frosting: Daddy, Mama, Luca, and everyone in my family. Then we went to Paris, collected our baby and Bruno's parents, Bapu and Moineau, and flew to New York. We stayed in a friend's apartment on West Tenth Street. It was icy cold in New York and my best friend, Connie, and I bought Luca a Gore-Tex blanket for his *pousette* in a tiny shop in the East Village. I wrapped him like an Indian papoose and only his little face stuck out, with his red cheeks. I felt safe. There was nothing in the world, I thought, that could happen to us.

When Luca was nearly four, we went back to Alsace. It was just before Christmas, but this was a darker time. Bruno had started on his "quest." I was confused and melancholy. We sat in restaurants and tried to talk, but when he explained himself, I stared at him in disbelief. He was not, I thought one afternoon, the same person I had married. He buried himself in novels by a spiritual French writer named Christian Bobin. I tried to read them and found it impossible: difficult phrases, unreasonable behaviour and ridiculous scenarios. Circus performers ran off with lovers. Men fell in love and became obsessed with dead women. The novels were about God, lonely journeys, men who spent their lives alone needing and wanting no one. Men who lived and died alone. The author himself, Bruno told me brightly, lived a solitary and simple life in the Burgundy countryside. He rarely saw anyone.

I hated Christian Bobin. I blamed him for this tsunami, this terrible and violent interference in my life.

We went back to the monastery and the chapel of angels, but I was miserable. We sat in a refectory with Christian pilgrims wearing handwoven sweaters and thick shoes, and I drank mulled wine alone, but there was no joy in it. We bought more gingerbread, and ordered *choucroute* the same way we had when we had come the first time, but in the middle of the meal, tears rolled down my face into my plate. Bruno said nothing: What could he say? I found, for the first time in my life—aside from when I had my tonsils out and had to be hospitalized—that I could not eat.

Once a week, together, we saw Irene. I grew to love her, her petite frame, and her New York–French accent. She was incredibly kind. Her apartment always smelled of food: good, sturdy winter food, which she said came from her neighbour who cooked all the time. Some afternoons I smelled stuffed peppers; other times it was roasted chicken. But the smell of food made me feel sick, as did the panic that gripped me in the stomach when we came out of the elevator door and into her apartment, the feeling that for one hour, we would be totally exposed.

Bruno talked a lot. He said things that made no sense, long stream-of-conscious sentences that left me raw. He smoked; he said things that shocked and surprised me; he spoke in phrases lifted from AA meetings. Even the impassive Irene occasionally lifted an eyebrow.

"It's a cult," I said.

"No, it's not a cult really," she said quietly. "But sometimes it replaces one addiction with another."

Christmas arrived. Bruno had always hated Christmas before I met him—it depressed him. He always was the one who volunteered to go to war zones over Christmas so other people could spend it with their families. Until Luca and I arrived, and then he spent hours threading coloured lights over the doors and the windows.

This year he had his studio. But he came home every day, saying, "This is *tellement difficile.*" He bought us a tree—despite the recession and my protests that we were broke—for 150 euros on the Boulevard Raspail. It looked Germanic and regal, and we draped the branches with the crystal and wooden ornaments that I had collected over the years. He spent hours decorating the window with fake snow and snowflake cut-outs. On the mirror above the fireplace, he sprayed two reindeer joined close together.

His mood pulled violently. He saw no one, went only to his AA meetings and spoke only to his sponsor. Some days he was lucid and kind, speaking in a calm and confident voice. Some days he came over and shook, and tears ran down his face. Some days I looked at him and did not recognize the person that looked back at me. He built fires and stared at them endlessly. He taught Luca how to build a fire, how to respect the fire, how to take care of the fire.

"Please don't let my son near the fire," I said.

"Nothing bad can happen when Daddy is here," he said. It was his mantra. He had started saying it the day we moved to Paris. But it sounded hollow. Because bad things had happened while he was there. I did my work and took care of my son. I read everything I could about alcoholics, spouses of alcoholics, children of alcoholics, sisters of drug addicts, dysfunctional families and post-traumatic stress disorder and war correspondents.

In the end, I gave up and decided I could only live by the rules that I knew. I tried to live joyfully, the way we had in the early days, even though I felt as though I had been burned alive. I played Christmas music in the early morning when I woke before Luca, and made him cinnamon toast and hot chocolate for breakfast. Then I roused him, warm and sleepy, his hair knotted around his shoulders, and carried him to the living room, wrapped in the striped blanket. Because of his sweet nature, or perhaps because Bruno and I constantly told him how much he was loved, he did not seem affected by this avalanche in our lives.

Those wintry mornings, I made and drank two dark coffees, then fed and dressed Luca in red wool sweaters and trousers for his Christmas show. Walking to school, in English, we sang "Jingle Bells," and "Santa Claus Is Coming to Town." But at school, in French, my little boy sang songs about *Père Noel*.

Over the years, Bruno gave me some very beautiful things. They were not things that you would see in magazine ads.

He bought me things that he took time to find, each one was individual and looked like me and came from places where he had been, and from when we were apart.

There were silver necklaces from Iraq inlaid with intricate pieces of lapis lazuli. There were silk evening gowns from Burma; midnight blue beads from Bamako; tunics that he said were "my colours" (deep olive green and blood red) that he spent hours wandering in a market in Karachi trying to find that would suit me. He found things that matched my eyes and my hair and my body.

Every time he brought me something, pulled it from his worn-out backpack, coming back from a trip like a Victorian adventurer, I saw the expression on his face as he passed the box or the bag to me. It was pride. He knew me. He saw me. Of the jewels, there were delicate rings that slipped over my fingers like pieces of silk; one from Los Angeles, one made from sapphires that he bought in Madagascar after he had been beaten up by a crowd, an emerald from somewhere else in Africa. There was a charm bracelet made from milky moonstones and pale green stones, my favourite beach colours. There was a necklace with a tiny circle, a symbol of love, hung by gold that he once gave a waitress to present to me with a glass of pink champagne on our anniversary. There was a diamond that fit around my wrist on a black cord with a note that said the colour indicated serenity.

The engagement ring itself was a beautiful thing. He had spent hours with the head of de Beers in Johannesburg, staring at stone after stone till he found this one. He had called me that day, excited. There was one that shone so much that it was magical, he said, but it was smaller than another which was equally startling, but bigger. He could not decide. "You choose," I said. He bought the bigger one and had it cut into a princess design. Because he said I was a princess.

But of all things he gave me, the thing I loved the most was my wedding ring. It was simple and gold, nothing elaborate, no diamonds or engraving. It was just a simple band, but when I wore it, it slid back and forth on my ring finger, the same long fingers my son would inherit, and the first thing his father saw when he popped outside of me, hands first. I loved that ring. It symbolized so much: stability after madness; settling down after roaming; softness after so much hardness. It meant we were a unit. The three of us.

Bruno understood me. He got me. The only decent line in the film *Avatar* is when one alien says to another: "I see you." Bruno saw me. No one else, I realized, in my entire life, ever had.

An Afghan friend once explained their mourning ritual: someone dies and for forty days the family mourns. They cry, they weep, they remember the dead, and they go through their days miserable and forlorn. They meet for lunch after prayers on Friday and recall the life and death of their loved one.

But on the forty-first day, life begins again. I decided that I had cried and mourned enough, that the funeral was over. It was my forty-first day.

One afternoon, in the early summer, I put the ring away in a cedar box that a friend who had died—from overdosing on a mixture of cocaine and heroin known as a speedball—

had given me for my thirtieth birthday. The box was rimmed with black and had a small key. Inside I put the diamond ring, the plastic man and wife from the top of our wedding cake, which had been a beautiful mound of caramel and crème anglaise, a *pièce montée*. I put a tiny note inside too, scented with the last of my Tocca perfume that he loved so much. The smell of happiness.

Love affair with Bruno, 1993–2009.

Last, I laid the wedding ring inside a tiny green leather box with a gold catch. I closed the box, locked it and put it on a shelf. Even as I was doing it, I realized it was dramatic, but it was something—a crazy, mad ritual—I had to perform.

Afterwards, I thought what other people would say: But why can't the two of you who love each other so much live together like normal people? Why can't you be, as the writer Isabel Allende once said, the kind of people who fit under the umbrella?

Because we weren't.

Long ago, when I met him, I knew Bruno was like Ulysses. He would roam the earth but would always yearn for home and mourn those whom he loved. But when he finally reached the home he wanted and needed, he would pace like a wounded tiger in a cage. He could not settle. He could not be settled. He had tried because of how much he loved me, and his son. But it was impossible, and it was killing me, and it was killing him to try.

Even after I locked his things in that box, he still brought me more gifts. A piece of rare green stone that hangs on a thick chain and changes colours in the sun, that matches the green in my eyes. A peace sign from Woodstock. Silk pyjamas from China.

My friend Bettina saw the green stone hanging around my neck and took it in her hands. "My God," she said solemnly, "he really sees you."

"I know." I said.

He saw me when he met me, in the lobby of the Holiday Inn on Sniper's Alley. And when he found me again, five years later, in a rose garden in Algiers. In a grimy pension in Jalalabad; a rooftop in St. Louis in Senegal; a seventh-floor walk-up near the Bastille; a lush garden overflowing with coconuts and mangoes in Abidjan; a Balinese bed on the Swahili coast of Kenya; a fluorescent-lit boarding house in Benin. And, finally, in the house he built to keep Luca and me safe, in Paris, near the Luxembourg Gardens.

And he sends me messages that no one else would understand. What do the messages say? They are always about love, but a certain kind of love. They are always about destiny, fate, surrendering. Redemption. They are always about us. "The promise I made to you in Sarajevo. I will never lose you." They are always about uncompromised emotion. "My tenderness is with you always."

At a party one night in London, I saw someone I knew from my other life. She said brightly and a little drunkenly, "Now that Luca is nearly six, will you go back on the road? You said you would."

I put down my paper cup of bad wine. "Did I? I don't remember."

But the next morning, I woke up and thought: *Now, it is time.* A few months later, I was on a Minnow helicopter in Helmand Province, Afghanistan, headed for a Forward Operating Base in Sangin to embed with British troops fighting a fierce battle against insurgents. The day I arrived was the memorial service for two soldiers killed the day before; one of them, Luke Farmer, was eighteen and a half years old. I thought of Luca at eighteen as I stared out the back of the helicopter at the brown and dusty Afghan landscape. I had always hated working in Afghanistan. Why was I back here?

The day before I left Paris I saw a clairvoyant on the rue Rambuteau. It was bitterly cold and the clairvoyant, who was from Haiti, was wrapped in a long sweater the colour of the sea. She made me a cup of Nescafé. She had just found out that an earthquake had struck her island that morning, but she did not yet know the gravity—that hundreds of thousands of people would die, and she would spend the rest of the day desperately trying to reach her father. "If the phone rings, I may have to answer it," she said, laying down her tarot cards.

I don't go to clairvoyants, but I went to see Malou because I wanted to know if I was going to die; if this trip to this remote army base in the most backward part of Afghanistan, a country already so backward that life and death practically intertwined, was going to be my last.

"I would like to know why you are going," my son's godfather asked me. It was hard to explain. Was it that I wanted my life back? The promise I had made long ago in the church at Our Lady of Victories, to give up everything, was I stealing back my promise, made in front of rows and rows of lit candles?

The clairvoyant was not sinister or remotely witchy. On the contrary, she was a French clairvoyant and decidedly chic with her high leather boots and her tight jeans. The trip, she said, staring at the cards in the wintry, frozen January light, was going to be difficult but important. "This is the beginning of a new life," she said. "I can't really tell you why, but it is."

I was in Afghanistan for nearly three weeks, and I came home a few days before Luca's sixth birthday. I stood by my son's bed, looking at his face. *Watch your son,* my friend Adam had always said to me. *Don't stop watching him.* That was his advice to me when I was in my darkest days. *Watch your son.* And my brother Richard's dying words: *Take care of your little boy.*

My little boy was bigger. He still looked angelic, but the fullness was leaving his cheeks. I was no longer terrified of being alone with him. I was no longer haunted by images of catastrophic disasters. I no longer hoarded water. I had finally abandoned the trauma of turning into a mother, to become a good mother. But he was growing up—and tragically—away from me. At night, reading *Peter Rabbit* to him, I tried desperately to hold him, as if to hold on to the years that were speeding by, too fast, too slippery for me to grasp.

As for his father, he was still lost in the world, seeking. We spoke to each other every day, from whichever country we were in, because we had both begun our voyages again. From Africa, where I lay in a bed open to the stars and watched the moon and swatted away mosquitoes and missed them both desperately; from Pakistan; from Kabul; from Dubai; from Libya and Egypt and Baghdad; from America; from Indonesia; and finally, from Sarajevo, the place where long, long ago we had met and fallen in love.

While there was deep sadness, there was no bitterness. We both knew we had given something incredible to each other, and out of the war, out of the violent teacher that had both tainted us and in some way damaged us for good, came this.

There was this child. Had Bruno not kissed me on the Pont des Artistes and run back and forth across the world, following me and running from me, this child would not be here. What we had given could never be taken away.

A friend tells me a story. The poet Robert Frost, late in his life, and already a hugely important poet, was asked by a student magazine to contribute a poem. The students could not afford to pay the famous poet, and they were intimidated to ask someone of his stature. But when they summoned the courage, Frost not only gave the poem, he said he believed that by giving it away, he would hold it closer to himself. He told them that anything strongly given is always kept.

EPILOGUE

Going Back

In what seemed like another lifetime, I met the love of my life in the lobby of a hotel in Sarajevo. Now it was fifteen years after the war had ended, fifteen years since Srebrenica where eight thousand men and boys were herded to their deaths, and fifteen years since the autumn day when my father died.

Everyone had forgotten what happened in this city, but I never wanted to forget, in the same way I never wanted to—and never would—forget what passed between Bruno and me. And so, one midwinter day, I went back to Sarajevo.

As the plane circled the thick, grey Balkan clouds, I heard a strange fairy-tale voice inside my head, and things I had long forgotten, I suddenly remembered. The story is this: once upon a time, in a place not so far away, a city on the

river, a city in Europe at the end of the twentieth century, a
medieval siege lasted for nearly three years.

It was a time of great darkness for the inhabitants, physically and mentally. Inside the city, which was surrounded by
mountains, there was no water, electricity, heating, petrol,
food or comforts. Packs of hungry wild dogs roamed the
street, picking up pieces of human flesh. Hundreds, sometimes thousands, of artillery shells fell on the city and on
the river, whose banks were smashed to pieces. Evil snipers perched on hillside mounts, taking aim at women and
children running across the street. Knees and thighs were
particularly vulnerable: easier to hit.

Surgeons operated by candlelight, or with miners' flashlights attached to their heads, and tried to keep their hands
steady as the artillery rocked the foundation of the buildings.
People burned their books to keep warm, and gathered twigs
in the city parks. The elderly died in their beds, freezing to
death, alone. An old man was shot between the eyes by a particularly accurate sniper. He had been chopping wood to
heat an old people's home that was on a front line that everyone—including the United Nations—forgot about.

As for the children of this siege, they learned to live with
fear, to comfort their parents during artillery attacks and to
understand madness. Schools stopped and time froze. There
were no birthday parties, no cakes made with fresh eggs, no
chocolate bars, no Christmas trees for the Christians or toys
for the Muslims at Bajram, no play dates or sing-a-longs.

And no one came to save these people, not for a long,
long time.

The bitter war continued, and in some way life went on. People made love and children were born. I held my baby godson in my arms at the Catholic cathedral one morning for his wartime baptism, and he screamed and screamed as water was poured on his head. Afterwards we celebrated with rice, bread, cake and chocolate bars bought in the black market. Those that lived through these awful days were bound together forever.

Everywhere I looked in Sarajevo on that return fifteen years later, I saw things in black and white, like a film, because of course the film was still being played in my head. I did not see the modern shopping centres or the pizza parlours or the internet cafés. I saw the sprits of the dead, which hung for me, like the low clouds that always hang over Balkan cities.

Gingerly, I went back to the Holiday Inn. There was the lobby, there was an elevator, now working, but I took the stairs, as I had always done during the war. In front of my old room, I saw all of my own dead, and all of my own memories, and my love story, my history with Bruno which had been built and played out behind that faded door. A long, long time ago, in a place far, far away.

The collective pain, the collective memory was everywhere. A psychiatrist in Kosevo Hospital, which stayed open during the siege and operated valiantly without electricity, even when the generators went off, once told me the city was a walking insane asylum at the height of the war.

Another told me that the best people had left the city or were killed.

Another told me to do myself a favour and move forwards, forget the past. Say *Dobje jenje Bosna.* Goodbye Bosnia.

But I wanted to remember. I cannot help but remember. It seemed imperative that after everything that had happened to me, I had to remember.

And so, coming back, flying from Ljubljana in the slick Slovenian jet cruising over Mount Igman, which once was the only exit route out of the siege, I looked down and tried to see the tunnel which had once been the only way to get supplies in and out of the city. I scanned the ground near Butmir, across from the landing strip of the airport, but could not see it.

I began to think of all I had lost, and all I had left behind, and I decided I must try to find—if he wanted to be found— Nusrat.

Long before Luca, long before I ever thought I could hold an infant in my arms, let alone become a mother, I had met Nusrat. He came into my life at a particularly insane time.

By the winter of 1993, I was beginning to go a little crazy, along with the three hundred thousand inhabitants of Sarajevo. The war that everyone thought would be over in a few weeks was dragging on in the brutal Balkan winter. The American flags that some families had hung from their frozen windows when a rumour went around the city that the Americans were coming to save them were beginning to look a little tattered, a little sad.

My friend Mario, a poet who had been caught in several artillery attacks, but survived, saw a woman's shoe full of blood in the snow one day. He rarely talked, but that day, he told me sombrely, "You can kill a life without killing anyone . . . you can take a city, but you don't snipe people, you don't butcher people, you don't burn down villages."

My friend Gordana saw a dog running with a human hand in its mouth. My friend Aida said, "We are all falling down Alice in Wonderland's rabbit hole." She remembers that first day of war in May 1992: she was walking down the street in her high heels and ponytail on her way to work when a tank came up behind her. As she crouched behind a trash can to take cover, she realized she was entering a new place from which she would probably never return.

Me too; I fell down a hole, a rabbit hole like Alice in Wonderland's, and never returned.

My room on the fourth floor of the Holiday Inn on Sniper's Alley had plastic windows that came from UNHCR humanitarian aid packets. On one side of the ugly, communist-era room was my flak jacket and my helmet, on my shrapnel-chipped "desk" was a battery-operated Tandy, a British-bought precursor to a laptop.

Physically, I was deteriorating. I had grown accustomed to not washing and I wore the same clothes several days in a row. I did not care. Oddly enough, even though no one washed in those days, no one seemed to smell. Once a week, I bribed the men who guarded the hotel kitchen with a few packs of Marlboro Lights for a pot of hot water, and with that, I would set aside an hour to laboriously wash my hair and my body. One night, in a fit of despair, I had chopped off my long, thick hair with a pair of borrowed manicure scissors. I did not want to be pretty.

My view out the plastic window was of a wasted, gutted city of burned-out buildings and metal canisters that were used to deter the snipers. It was so cold that my skin peeled off in dry patches when I took off my layers of clothes. I was living on a diet of chocolate bars, whisky and cigarettes I had brought in from Kiseljak, the Las Vegas–style frontier town which was the last stop before besieged Sarajevo.

To this day, I cannot forget that cold. The large, cavernous Soviet-style unheated rooms where we would interview doctors or politicians; the freezing cold houses where people sat huddled and frightened around an oil stove; the ugly interior of the lobby of the Holiday Inn, where one afternoon I came back to see journalists abseiling down from the roof with ropes.

I shivered when I woke in my sleeping bag, I shivered when I climbed out and slipped into the same clothes that I had left on the floor the night before, and I shivered climbing back into the bag at night, to read by candlelight. Bizarrely, maids came every day to make up the beds—that is, to pat down the sleeping bags, and to move around the dust. There was not much they could do without water. The toilets did not flush and no water came out of the taps.

I was mentally fried. Every day people came to me with some kind of request: get me out of here, smuggle a package to my sister, take my child to Germany, and give me some money for firewood. The worst was the knowledge that I could leave whenever I wanted to, and they could not.

To compensate for the madness, I had some little routines that kept me sane, like someone stricken with obsessive compulsive disorder. One was to visit the morgue, every day. I usually did this in the morning, when Aliya Hadzic, a pleasant Muslim man in his early fifties who ran the morgue, would still be in a talkative mood. By the time I arrived, Aliya would have counted the dead who came in overnight from the front lines and the hospitals, closed their eyes, tried to straighten their limbs, or if there were no limbs, he would try to piece together the ravages of an artillery or sniper attack.

"Everyone else was afraid of the dead," he would tell me later. "But I never was. The dead cannot hurt you."

After he arranged the bodies on slabs, and closed their eyes, he then took out an ordinary notebook and carefully wrote down the names of the dead. This was important. Aliya is a simple man, born in eastern Bosnia, a farmer at heart, but he took his job seriously and he believed that the dead deserved some respect, especially during war. So he wrote down their names, and where the bodies had arrived from, in simple school notebooks. By the end of the war, there was a stack of twenty-eight notebooks, some brown, some green, some bound with yellowing scotch tape.

If the dead had been killed in an attack in the city, he wrote *grad*. If they had died after being treated in the hospital, he wrote the unit they came from—*C3* meant surgery.

Soldiers were given names of the front lines where they were killed—Stup, Otes, Zuc—and you could always tell where the fighting was heaviest overnight by how many were killed. There were a few NIs written down—*Nema Imena,* person unknown.

Aliya did not fear the corpses; he prepared them for their funerals, but his assistant, Ramzic, was afraid. The poor man drank himself into a stupor just to do his job, and even then, he did not do it well enough, according to Aliya.

"It was no use having Ramzic around," he said. "I might as well have worked alone." Once, when the electricity worked at Kosevo Hospital—a rare occurrence—the two men had to go to a top floor to collect some bodies. The power went out, and they were stuck for hours. Ramzic stunk of booze.

"I kept asking him why he did it, why he was drinking himself to death," Aliya said. "I did the same work and I did not have to drink to do it."

But Ramzic looked at him woefully. "What can I do?" he said. "It's a war."

This was a common expression in Sarajevo during the siege. Every possible question, from "Why don't you love me any more?" to "Why are you cheating on your wife?" was answered with the same response: "What we can do? It's a war." It was a refrain repeated over and over by priests, doctors, soldiers, commanders, politicians, aid workers, mothers, teachers. They all said the same thing: "What we can do? It's a war."

I remember Ramzic well. He was bad-tempered and day

by day appeared to grow more nutty. He was certainly always drunk. But he survived. He did not get hit by the snipers that aimed at people running across Marsala Tito Street. He missed all the shells that hit the centre of the city.

But he killed himself a few years after the war, hanged himself with a rope. Aliya is not really sure why, but he reckons the alcohol, the memory of those dead bodies and probably a bad love affair finally got to Ramzic.

Some days at the morgue were worse than others. During the first months of the war, Aliya remembers fifty or sixty people being brought in a day. There were the terrible days of massacres—the bread-line massacre, the water-line massacre, the market massacres—these were days when people went out to get food or supplies and got targeted, deliberately, by Serbs.

There were days when children were brought in, groups of them. Aliya hated those days. That was when the children went outside to play, like one snowy morning, because they could not bear to sit in their apartments any more. You can see the scene: the tired, frightened mother, her children begging her to go outside for some fresh air. So they go, because really, no one but a monster would send an artillery shell into a group of kids building a snowman.

But they did. Aliya was there the day the children came in from Ali Pashe Polje, the kids who were playing in the snow, and died from it. He hated that day.

But the worst day of all was the day he came in and found his son, his beloved son, his oldest son, the boy who could do anything, lying dead on the slab. Ibrahim. Twenty-three years old, about to become a father in three months. A military policeman. Aliya was late to work that day. He remembers he took his breakfast, some bread that tasted like sawdust and some tea, and wandered down the hill from his house, avoiding the usual places that snipers could see.

When he climbed the hill towards Kosevo, and made his way to the morgue, he saw a crowd outside. *What's this?* he thought, getting impatient. *What do they want?* Then he saw people he knew, some of his son's friends. *It's Ibrahim,* he thought, and went into the morgue. He saw his son, dead. He remembers that everything went black. "I just passed out," he says.

Eighteen years later, I find Aliya and he recognizes me instantly. He is retired and he now lives on a hill above Sarajevo in a house he once built for his son. He tends his cows, because cows are easier than the dead. He is now sixty-four and could have worked a few extra years, but he feels that he has seen enough.

We leave the cows and sheep and go to his house and his wife, whose face is still etched with pain, makes us fresh juniper juice and heavily sugared Bosnian coffee. We sit, and we talk, and he remembers everything; the death of his son, that day, that time.

But something good came of it. His daughter-in-law gave birth to a little boy a few months after Ibrahim was buried. The little boy is now seventeen. He looks just like his father did, and Aliya can sometimes squint his eyes a bit and pretend it is his lost son.

But still, that day that he found his firstborn child, his

boy, lying on a slab in his morgue was the worst day of his life.

My wartime routine rarely varied. Around midday, I made my way up the hill of Bjelave to the Ljubica Ivezic orphanage. This was a strange and terrible place.

When the war started, everyone had seemed to run away except the donkey-faced director, Amir Zelic. I did not like him, nor he me, but for some reason, he would let me in and allow me to poke around. There were some days he kicked me out, but most of the time he seemed not to care. He asked me for cigarettes and disappeared.

Sometimes Amir was there, sometimes he was not, but no matter what, the children ran completely wild. Not only were they abandoned or orphaned, but many of them were mentally incompetent. When the shelling started, or when it happened at night—particularly terrifying, because there was no electricity so they lay in the dark with the whistle of the shells getting closer—they howled like dogs.

There were some older, truly crazed kids there, and one wintry day, they locked me in a room for a few hours and I had to climb out through a skylight. If you approached them, they wanted cigarettes, money, drugs and food. They shouted: "Fuck you, bitch! Welcome to hell! Whore! Fuck you!"

The little ones seemed to get completely lost in the shuffle. They were dirty, smelly and pitiful. If you tried to hold them, they flinched. I never knew, but I am sure, there was terrible abuse going on when no one was looking—which was more or less all the time.

To eat, there was rice and strawberry yogurt powder twice a day, which Amir would proudly show me. There were rats, and rain poured through the broken windows. The floors were oily and damp, and it smelled. The children slept eight or nine to a room on piles of rags or clothes. There were no toilets, and they scratched with dirt and lice and neglect.

One day I found Nusrat Krasnic. He was nine, and looked more like a wild animal than a little boy. He was a Roma child—the Roma make up 5 per cent of the Bosnian population—and had dark, matted hair and rather beautiful eyes. He was skinny as a rail, and dressed in thin cotton clothes in the middle of winter. His boots were passed on by someone who left or died, and they were too big. What I remember the most—and what hurt me the most—was that he wore socks on his hands in the middle of the biting, savage winter.

His mother and father had died during the war, in their house on Sirokaca Street. He had two brothers, and somehow they ended up at the orphanage at the beginning of the war—Amir was not sure how. "I can't keep track of these kids. It's a war!" he said gruffly when I tried to get information on his family. Someone said his father might still be alive, and I went back to Sirokaca Street and asked around. No one had seen him. "But he's a gypsy. They move around. Even during war."

This is what we knew: Nusrat's mother, Ljubica, was killed when a shell crashed through the wall of the kitchen and reduced the entire house to a pile of rubble. Nusrat knew the house was trashed, but at least once a week, he tried to get back. He ran away from the orphanage, and made the dangerous trek, crossing front lines and going too close to snipers to get back home. Once he got pinned down for more than an hour, hiding inside a flowerpot on a bridge as a firefight raged around him.

Nusrat knew things, which he shared with me on long, cold wintry days when we walked through the city together. He knew about *grenatas*—grenades—and what size they were. He knew how to jump on trucks and steal humanitarian aid packages to get extra food, and how to sell it. He knew what sniffing glue was, because the big kids in the orphanage did it. And he knew that somewhere there was some kind of love: at night, he slept wrapped around his dog, Juju.

I forgot sometimes that he was a kid, because he was more like an old man. But he was only nine years old, and he still had it in him to want to play. So he and his brother, Mohammed, went sledding in the snow by grabbing onto UN trucks that passed and sliding along behind them.

Once in a while, he took me to the basement of the Hotel Europe, which had been bombed to pieces during the summer of 1992. Before the war, during the Hapsburg Empire, it had been the fashionable hotel for the well-heeled doing a Balkan tour. Inside the so-called Golden Visitor's Book I found a page inscribed in 1907 by ancestors of a Bostonian friend: *Mrs. H. H. H. Hunnewell. Wellesley, USA.*

But more than eighty years later, the place was akin to hell. Luckier refugees found bombed-out rooms and moved their meagre possessions inside, guarding their space jealously. The less fortunate hovered in the basement, which was full of water. Nusrat had some friends down there. An older refugee woman had taken in Nusrat and his brother, and tried to guide them.

The war had turned Nusrat savage. I tried to feed him, give him clothes and shoes, and some tenderness, but I was aware always that I was temporary: that I would go, and he would be back on the streets. One day, I sat down with him and a book, but Nusrat had not been to school in a long, long time; not since before the war. He had forgotten how to write his name.

One day, I left for a month to rest. I flew back to London and went to cocktail parties where people always asked the same question: What is it like to get shot at? But I could not enjoy myself in London, even with the marvel of hot water that ran through pipes. I stood under showers for an hour, till my skin rubbed raw from the heat. I ate real food, vegetables and fruit, and went into shops and remembered what it was like to have newspapers and telephones.

But then I thought of Nusrat and my friends inside the siege, and I felt terribly guilty. I bought him clothes for the summer, and vitamins and food. But when I returned in late April, when the water in the river was rushing high, and the spring military offensive was in full flow, and the Serbs were really kicking the shit out of Sarajevo, Nusrat had disappeared.

When I came back I didn't stay at the Holiday Inn, but in the Hotel Europa. I took an elevator to the basement. The place where Nusrat and I huddled in the cold is now a gym with an elliptical machine and a sauna. There is a pool. The breakfast table was full too—sausages, eggs, bread and all different kinds of cheeses, imported meats. German businessmen crowd the table, stuffing their plates with rolls and honey. It almost hurts to look at the waste, remembering how the people I loved had hoarded a box of powdered milk, a tin of beef.

And I began my hunt for Nusrat.

No one seems to know where he is. The donkey-faced director, Amir Zelic, is still there, and he sends me a message through Velma, my interpreter: no Nusrat. Apparently, he stayed at the orphanage until five years ago—which would have made him twenty-four when he left—and no one has seen him since. The police have no record of his coming, or going.

But I am sceptical of Amir, because he was involved in a scandal at the orphanage a few years earlier. There was a terrible fire and eight babies perished. No one seems to know the details, but Amir was under investigation, so is wary of talking to the press.

After the war, nuns from Zagreb restored the Dickensian building to a beautiful white convent with hard, glistening wood throughout. It smells of lemon oil. The nuns were neat and clean and took care of children in need. One Sunday morning, I sit with one of the sisters and she tells me that they have tried to scour most of the memories of the war away. She shows me the neat chapel, the fresh flowers.

But on the other side of the building, they moved the

wild kids, and Amir was still in charge. People heard about the orphanage during the war, and with donor money, they rebuilt it and the rooms where the children sleep are now clean and light and full of toys. There is a room of babies, smiling, beautiful, fat babies.

The morning I go to meet Amir, two men who guard the door tell me they know Nusrat well.

"He was here last week," they said. "He comes sometimes for breakfast."

But the last time they saw him, Nusrat was in terrible shape. He was homeless, and had taken to begging in the new parking lot in front of the Sanpaolo Banka. He spent the night outside, and the men told me they thought he was taking drugs. His brother, Mohammed, who had taken care of him in the orphanage (more or less) had died a few months earlier, from an overdose.

"He seems very ashamed of his life now," one of the men told me. "We tell him to come, have a shower, have a meal, but he only shows up once in a while."

"When he is really desperate," says the other man. They take my cell phone number and promise to call me if Nusrat comes back, and they tell me where to go to look for him.

Oh, Nusrat, I failed you, I thought quietly while waiting for Amir. When he came down the stairs, he recognized me, and I him, immediately.

"Oh, it's you," he said.

"Long time," I answered.

"Fifteen years," he said, rubbing his girth. He had gotten fatter but otherwise looked the same. He called for hibiscus tea, coffee. A plate of biscuits appeared. He said he had gotten divorced. "Who knows why? The war did terrible things to all of us."

"And Nusrat?" I asked.

Amir nodded. Nusrat came in from time to time, he said, but he never stayed the night. He had been at the home until he was in his early twenties. The death of his brother had been a blow.

Was he also taking drugs?

Amir shrugged. "Most likely. I tried to get him a job a while back, and he failed all the drug tests."

I remembered the skinny kid who showed me how to hook a hand over the back of the UN trucks and slide, slide, slide.

"What can you do?" he said, and I froze, thinking he was going to say, "It's a war." Instead he said, "We could not save all of them." We went up to see the babies, but Amir was in a rush. He would not let me hold any of them, even though they were all so very beautiful.

One day, during the war, Nusrat showed me a secret room in the orphanage, a room that was magically heated with oil heaters, and where there were several women in clean clothes. Inside this room, there were also tiny babies.

We snuck inside, Nusrat and me, when the ladies were not there, and I held these babies. I sat in a chair, and inexperienced with children, shifted the infants from one shoulder to the next. Nusrat sat on the floor grinning. And that became another of our rituals: waiting until the ladies went to do something else, sneaking inside and holding the babies.

They were warm and smelled clean. I began to feel something I had never felt before: maternal.

But one day we got caught, and the big woman in a white dress with those strange Eastern European clogs they wear in Bosnia kicked us out. She locked the door behind her, and told me if she caught me again near that room, she would tell Amir and he would ban me from the premises.

Later that day, Nusrat told me a secret. Those were the babies of the Muslim women who were touched. Meaning raped. The women who had been held in rape camps in Foca and other places east of Sarajevo, and raped and raped and raped, until they became pregnant. An attempt, someone once told me, to wipe out their gene pool. And this is partially where that terrible phrase—ethnic cleansing—came from.

I found one of those rape babies when she was eight. Marina. She was so beautiful, like an angel. I kept staring at her perfect, tiny, lovely face, unable to imagine that such a child could come from an act so violent. She went to school and had no idea her father was one of perhaps a dozen men who held her mother in a sports hall in Foca and raped her and raped her and raped her.

While Marina was playful and sweet and was told her father was a war hero killed during a battle, her mother was not so joyful. She was a train wreck of a human being, more a shell of a body wearing a tracksuit than an actual person. Her soul seemed to have been squeezed from her.

She shook and cried, she was full of shame and rage, and she took tranquillizers to sleep and pills to fuel her up during the day. She rarely ate. And yet she still tried to protect her daughter, a child she had once wanted to abort because of the seed that had made her. But at the last minute, she realized the baby was half hers. We went for a pizza and sat silently. Marina told me she liked cartoons: because it was not the real world.

One early spring day after I see Amir, I go to see Jasna. Jasna was in that hall with Marina's mother those awful days in the summer of 1992 in Foca, but she did not have a baby. She did not have a baby because when she was raped, over and over, nine times by her count, she was only twelve years old and did not yet have her period.

Her mother was raped alongside her on one of the occasions. Neither mother nor daughter could help the other. The little girl screamed at the pain of losing her virginity to a soldier three times her age, and her mother was powerless to help her. Afterwards, when they brought them back to the sports hall, they did not look at each other, and they never talked about it.

Today Jasna is thirty. She is a widow; her husband, a manual worker, died three years ago, electrocuted on a job. She cannot bear children; she tried for several years and the doctors told her to give up. Meanwhile, we keep looking for Nusrat.

Every day, my interpreter Velma and her boyfriend drive to the parking lot late at night to look for Nusrat. But they never find him.

I can't forget you, Nusrat, I think. *If I forget you, then it seems so much has been in vain.* Instead, I go to see the man who knows best about memory: Aliya, and his book of the dead.

We meet again early on a Friday morning, the Muslim day of prayer and first day of the weekend, in a cemetery past the tunnel where one of the few Bosnian tanks used to hide, draped in camouflage. He's waiting for me, squinting in the sunlight, wearing city clothes rather than his farming clothes: a neat pair of corduroys, a brown sweater and a checked shirt. He takes me inside the office of the cemetery.

There are twenty-four books of the dead, and we begin at the beginning: July 1992, his first day at work, when he took over the job at the morgue. His hands, big and calloused, used to dealing with the skin of his cows rather than the skin of the dead, open the first book. He sits down, with great and heavy exhaustion, and sighs. He opens the book, which already, only fifteen years after the war, seems very old.

The books are neat and orderly. He goes through them one by one, telling me about the things he remembers.

"This was my neighbour . . . ," he says as he points to one name. At another line, he drops his head. "This was a young girl."

Finally, he gets to a page in October 1992. He takes out his handkerchief. He wipes his eyes. He runs his big, calloused, farmer's hands over the page. His eyes blur. "And this is my son."

I have always been close to the dead. Perhaps it is because I have lost so many people I love. Like Aliya, I am not afraid of the dead. I dream of them all, with alarming frequency. Once in a dream, my father was wearing wrinkled pyjamas. This was unusual, because he was an impeccably groomed man. He was wandering the streets, in his pyjamas, looking lost. Maybe it's all a mistake that he is dead.

"You're dead, Daddy," I said. "Go away."

He looked hurt. "Who told you I'm dead? I'm just in the next room."

I have often thought we are connected to the dead, like the bridges that span the River Miljaka, like the bridge on which Prince Ferdinand was shot in Sarajevo, commencing the Great War. I think sometimes we never lose the dead. I believe strongly we must never forget them. During the war, I used to read the Anne Sexton poem "The Truth the Dead Know" over and over, as if it had a clue to the insanity that was killing the city of Sarajevo. I loved her poem, how she referred to the dead without shoes, in their stone boats. I understood her description of the remoteness, the heaviness, of death.

I am losing my memory, as the war fades further away from me.

I ask my friend Louie to help me remember.

I love Louie. He was a soldier, my friend, a tall, thin Serb from Sarajevo who fought on the Bosnian side. He was never a comforter—he was too gruff for that—but he was someone I knew I could trust with my life. He says, "No one ever touched you during the war because of me."

When I would feel totally alienated sometimes out of fear or loneliness or desperation, he would take me to strange places with strange people—gangsters, probably—where they had a bottle of whisky. Then we would smoke and drink, and he would say, "Feel better? Now go home." He would drive me home and walk me to my door.

When I see him now, he is so much, much older. He shakes. He drinks a lot. He is so sad, a sadness that I know you cannot wash away with years. What is it you saw? Did you taste fear in your mouth like metal, and what did you smell? Those first days of war when you and your friends tried to hold off the tanks with Kalashnikovs, when you gathered at a factory out near the airport, a small virtually helpless band of kids trying to fight off Goliath, what did you think?

So Louie and I return on my last day in the new Sarajevo to all the places of the dead. To the front lines where he fought, eighteen years ago, He has never been back, and at some moments while we stare silently at the buildings where he crouched with a gun, at the factory where the battle raged for more than twenty-four hours, I am thinking perhaps it was not a good idea to bring him back.

"My nerves," he says to me. "Now you wonder why I shake so much?"

We stand on a railway bridge in Otes, a suburb of Sarajevo, and he looks like he will cry. "We had no guns," he says, "we had only rifles that cost one hundred deutschmarks, and we tried to take the guns from the dead soldiers . . ." We look down at a muddy, polluted creek.

At the Jewish cemetery, the scene of some of the heaviest fighting, where the men fought from headstone to headstone, someone has built a new house. A sparkling *Architectural Digest* house that leans out over the city heights, with a view of Sarajevo below. It must belong to someone who was not here during the war of course—if he was, he would not live here, amongst so many dead, so many lingering dead.

Then we go to Dobrinja. It was a wild place, a suburb cut off from the rest of the city for most of the war, where the fighting was always intense. I remember days of shelling, of sitting with people screaming from fear and pain, of running across fields of snow with soldiers urging me to run faster, run faster, reporter, run faster . . .

In Dobrinja—where transporters opened up on the civilians on 4 May 1992 and a loudspeaker urged the people to take hand luggage and leave (not many of the population of forty-five thousand did), Louie fought hand to hand. He was what they call a defender of the city.

But when we go back, there is a terrible moment when neither of us can remember anything. We go back to the main street—now called Branilaca Dobrinje, Defenders of Dobrinja—but we can't recognize anything.

Instead of a wasted, grey outlay of communist-style buildings eaten away by tank shells and dead faces, and people running from snipers, there are pizza parlours, a playground, gold shops, gangs of beautiful teenagers smoking cigarettes, a sports hall and dogs rolling in the early spring sun.

"My God," Louie says. There are tears in his eyes. "I can't . . . remember anything. I can't see where we were . . ."

He climbs out of his car and lights a cigarette. He is growing agitated. He is shaking again. He stares at the buildings, looking a little desperate.

I can't remember either. I can't recognize where we once stood. But wait—isn't that the building I sprinted from with a soldier who was taking me to the front line, holding my hand as we ran? No, it can't be. And isn't that basement the old Bosnian army headquarters? The room where I saw that ancient woman who was dying of the cold? The place where the children were killed . . . the snow banks, the trenches, the sandbags used as defences, the metal canisters . . .

Everything has changed. Everything and nothing.

"Let's go," Louie says quietly. "I don't want to remember anyway."

A few months later, I finally found Nusrat. We met in a café not far from the Holiday Inn, and I fought back tears as this little boy emerged, now a man, carrying two plastic sacks, everything he owned inside them.

He was homeless. He lived on the streets. His brother, Mohammed, was dead, perhaps of an overdose. And Nusrat himself had suffered brutally in the aftermath of the war: he had stayed in the orphanage until he was twenty-four, then married a girl he met inside it. They had a child. The child was one of the infants killed in the fire.

He looked away, tears stinging his dark eyes, and I remembered how pained I was when he was a little boy, orphaned, and wearing socks on his hands instead of mittens.

You can't save the world, Bruno had always told me when I came back from assignments, gutted and wasted from helplessness, the intensity of pain other people lived through. You can't save people. You've got to grow a thicker skin.

But Nusrat could have been saved, I was sure of it. Somehow he seemed to epitomize every lost boy I had ever encountered in my life: my brothers, my husband. And now, in the café, he ordered a tea, but politely declined food. He said he slept outdoors most nights, and begged in a parking lot outside a bank. His war memories, like mine, were getting dimmer.

I went to other places in my life, but I never fell in love with a place again like I did with Sarajevo, the same way I will never love anyone again, I am sure, the way I love Bruno.

Both were linked to me forever. The city on the river captivated me, held me, haunted me, the same way he did. I did try to exorcize them both. Sarajevo was easier. One day, in a fit of madness, I burned every single notebook I had used to report the siege, page by page, in a fire in a friend's garden. As the pages went up in smoke, I hoped, I thought, I was burning the worst of the memories from myself. My tattoo of my worst pain.

But I did not. I never could. Once upon a time, a long long time ago, in a city on the river, during the month of May when there was nothing to eat but cherries that fell from the trees, I met a soldier.

He was very young—twenty-one—and very beautiful,

and when he ran along the front lines near the river, he loped, like a wolf. He was fast, a sprinter, and before the war he was a student of journalism and politics. His eyesight was perfect, and so they gave him a gun and made him a sniper.

We loved each other. It was not the kind of love where you run away together and get married and have children and live happily after. It was the kind of unconsummated love between two people who had fallen through the rabbit hole and had gone mad with war, drunk with war. We lived together, as comrades, in an apartment on a front line so vicious that we heard the shells crashing and throbbing, and sometimes it was so insane that I thought I heard him laughing and laughing. But later he told me he was crying.

Many years later we meet in the new, spanking clean Hotel Europa. He is not a boy. He has an MBA and works in a bank. After the war, he spent years abroad, trying to forget. He is a father; I am a mother. He wants to live in Dubai, get rich.

When we hug each other, it is the touching of two strange survivors. We always tell each other we love the other. On 11 September 2001, he found me somehow, and rang me on my cell phone—I was in Paris getting a visa to go to Afghanistan—and said: "I love you." What he meant, I guess, was that his country had been destroyed and now mine was too.

We both never forgot Sarajevo.

"That war broke my heart," I once told him.

"That war broke my everything," he responded. "The only good thing that happened is that I met you."

On my last day in Sarajevo, I tell my friend about Nusrat.

He lights a cigarette and tells me maybe there are times for remembering, and maybe there are times for forgetting, and this is a time for forgetting.

Later, I ask him what happened to this city, because perhaps it was some clue about what happened to me.

Long, long ago, in a place far away . . . why did the people rip each other to pieces? And why was it so linked to my own life?

He listens to me patiently. "You should let it go," he says finally. "Let it all go. Just try to live a happy life, as happy as you can possibly be. We are not as broken as you think," he says.

He gets up to take his long, handsome coat. He cups my face in his hands. He kisses me goodbye. He goes through the door of the Hotel Europa, into the new world, perhaps even more frightening than the comfortable world of the war, and I know he is, like me, forgetting and remembering.

THANK YOU:

Luca and Bruno, without whom there would be no story, no light.

To William Callahan at Inkwell Management, who first read this book, and with the eye of a master, helped me structure and build it.

To Alba Arikha and Susannah Hunnewell, who gave me the confidence to be a better mother, who did not laugh at my fears, who sat with me for hours in emergency rooms and cafés, who told me how to cut babies' nails and drink gin martinis.

Wendell Steavenson, who listened, and cooked, and listened and cooked, and cooked and listened.

ACKNOWLEDGMENTS

To Anna Seassau and Catherine Rubin, who patiently taught me how to be a Parisian Mama, and who always laid a plate for me and Luca at their kitchen tables.

For Raquel Ramos Bundalian and Leis Montero, Luca's beloved nannies. For my parents-in-law Marie-Louise and the late Philippe Girodon, who always treated me like a real daughter. For Adam Phillips, for the patient, painful unravelling.

And for my mother, Kathryn Buccino di Giovanni, who finally became my dearest friend and confidante when I became a mother.

This book took six years to write. Any other editor or agent would have lost confidence in me long ago. So eternal thanks to Kim Witherspoon, David Godwin, David Forrer, Ash Green and Alexandra Pringle, for waiting. And to Andrew Carlson, whose patience was often tested.

To Julia Reed, who believed and believed.

And for Cindy and Oswaldo Fumei, who brought me to Lamu, gave me a bed in front of the Indian Ocean and a library in Corsica, and allowed me the peace and quiet to finish this book.

And for L. R., who brought me back from the dead.

AUTHOR'S NOTE

It is difficult to write about members of your family, people you love the most in the world, when they are still living. So I would like to say that all the important characters in this book—Bruno Girodon, my mother, Ariane Quentier and others—read it before it was published and gave me their blessing. It was especially difficult for Bruno, who is the most private of individuals, to read the story of his crash and burn but his eventual triumph and sobriety. It is just one more example of his courage. He said, even if he did not agree with ways I had described events: "I would not dream of changing a word. This is your story to tell and you must tell it."

Bruno always said to me when I was under some bomb-ing raid, and he wanted to reassure me: "The best journalist is the one who gets out alive to tell the story." To tell this story, I had to live it, often with pain, to the end.

Janine di Giovanni
Paris, March 2011

A NOTE ON THE TYPE

This book was set in Adobe Garamond. Designed for the Adobe Corporation by Robert Slimbach, the fonts are based on types first cut by Claude Garamond (c. 1480–1561). Garamond was a pupil of Geoffroy Tory and is believed to have followed the Venetian models, although he introduced a number of important differences, and it is to him that we owe the letter we now know as "old style." He gave to his letters a certain elegance and feeling of movement that won their creator an immediate reputation and the patronage of Francis I of France.

Typeset by Scribe,
Philadelphia, Pennsylvania
Designed by Virginia Tan